P

2000

With love to Bill, Jean, Rob and Shani

This is the third year that I've written these books and it's about time I thanked all the people who help me to put them together. I have worked with some of them since the beginning of the books, and others have only recently started lending me their help, but I am immensely grateful to them all. So thank you, Nova Jayne Heath, Nicola Chalton, Nick Robinson and everyone else at Robinson Publishing for being such a great team to work with. Thanks to Chelsey Fox for all her agenting skills. And a huge thank you to Annie Lionnet and Jamie Macphail for their tireless work.

PISCES
2000

Jane Struthers

First published in 1999 by Parragon

Parragon
Queen Street House
4 Queen Street
Bath BA1 1HE
UK

Produced by Magpie Books, an imprint of
Robinson Publishing Ltd, London

© Jane Struthers 1999

Illustrations courtesy of Slatter-Anderson, London

ISBN 0 75252 901 3

A copy of the British Library Cataloguing-in-Publication Data
is available from the British Library

Printed and bound in the EC

CONTENTS

Dates for 2000

Pisces 19 February – 19 March

Aries 20 March – 18 April

Taurus 19 April – 19 May

Gemini 20 May – 20 June

Cancer 21 June – 21 July

Leo 22 July – 21 August

Virgo 22 August – 21 September

Libra 22 September – 22 October

Scorpio 23 October – 21 November

Sagittarius 22 November – 20 December

Capricorn 21 December – 19 January

Aquarius 20 January – 18 February

YOUR PISCES SUN SIGN

This chapter is all about your Sun sign. I'm going to describe your general personality, as well as the way you react in relationships, how you handle money, what your health is like and which careers suit you. But before I do all that, I want to explain what a Sun sign is. It's the sign that the Sun occupied at the time of your birth. Every year, the Sun moves through the sky, spending an average of 30 days in each of the signs. You're a Piscean, which means that you were born when the Sun was moving through the sign of Pisces. It's the same as saying that Pisces is your star sign, but astrologers prefer to use the term 'Sun sign' because it's more accurate.

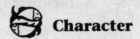 **Character**

Pisces is the last of the twelve signs of the zodiac, and it's said to contain a little of each of the other eleven signs. Some people even believe that a soul's last incarnation is always under the sign of Pisces. We have no way of knowing whether that's true, but Pisces is certainly the sign of the saint or the sinner or both rolled into one. The glyph for Pisces represents two fish swimming in opposite directions, and this illustrates the way Pisces can hit the heights or sink to the lowest depths. It's a sign of two extremes.

Because you're ruled by the nebulous planet Neptune you have an other-worldly quality that can make it difficult for you to keep your feet on the ground. And your Water element means you are easily swayed by your emotions. The result is that Pisces is the sign of the dreamer, the visionary and the mystic, but it can also be the sign of the fantasist and the criminal, thanks to Neptune's capacity for escapism and deception.

Reality is a very difficult concept for you to come to terms with. You have an instinctive dislike of unpleasant situations or harsh facts, and try to put as much distance between them and yourself as possible. This may simply mean that you're reluctant to watch violent films or read unsavoury articles in the newspapers, or it may make you view life through rose-coloured glasses, ultimately deceiving yourself into believing things are much better than they really are the results can be disastrous. If you want to be truly happy, you must learn to temper your need for peace and harmony with an ability to face up to life as it really is, warts and all.

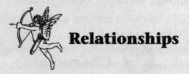 **Relationships**

Your emotions are always near the surface and you often wear your heart on your sleeve. And what a huge heart you have, which makes you a born romantic but also very sensitive and vulnerable to possible hurt and pain. It also makes you extremely emotional, and you pour out love and affection to your favourite people. If you're lucky, your loved ones are able to respond in kind or to accept your love without feeling overwhelmed. Even so, you should try to keep your feelings in check if they threaten to spiral out of control too often. Some signs simply can't cope with a lot of emotional drama, with the result that you could end up being hurt.

It's natural for you to see the best in other people, which is one of the reasons you have so many admirers. However, it also puts you at risk of potential heartbreak because it makes you blind to a loved one's failings. Even if everyone else can see that someone is no good for you, you'll persist in ignoring their faults and trusting that love will find a way. When it does, you're deliriously happy. When it doesn't, you sink to the depths of despair.

Money

Given your reluctance to face up to unpleasant truths, it's highly likely that you'd prefer to skip reading this section altogether. Pisces and money go together like oil and water, especially when it comes to the day-to-day management of your finances. If you're a typical Piscean who concentrates all your energies on creative activities rather than materialistic ones, your heart probably plummets every time you think about your finances. You may find it difficult to keep track of where all the money goes to, or may get into a real state whenever it's time to tackle your taxes.

Although you may dream sometimes of a wonderfully lavish lifestyle, you're probably perfectly happy if you have enough money to live on, preferably with a little left over to give to your loved ones. All the same, it's a good idea to set aside any spare cash for a rainy day or a big treat, but make sure you get sound, independent financial advice before doing this. Because you're so trusting, it's easy for sharks and con-men to get the better of you, so be very cautious when investing your money and don't be talked into taking risks that you can't afford.

 **Health**

With your emotions so close to the surface, it's no wonder that they often spark off strange health concerns. Very often Piscean illnesses are caused by emotional problems rather than germs and bacteria. Stress can present particular problems for you because it can play havoc with your extremely sensitive nervous system, triggering such symptoms as headaches, stomach upsets and sleepless nights. Take immense care of yourself, making sure you don't skimp on meals and that you get plenty of rest. Whenever you feel particularly vulnerable you should try to keep away from tense or unpleasant atmospheres, because you can soak up negative vibrations like a psychic sponge. You may even find that you come out in sympathy whenever someone describes their illness. Be especially careful of people who've always got a tale of woe to tell, because they'll affect you deeply.

The feet are the most vulnerable area for a Piscean, so you may suffer from corns, chilblains or find it difficult to find shoes that fit properly. Whenever you feel tense, treat yourself to a pedicure or give yourself a foot massage, which will help to clear any build-up of negative energy. You might also be allergic to certain foods or drugs, and may respond much better to some complementary medicines than prescription drugs.

Career

Your dual Piscean nature really comes into its own here, because your sign is drawn to professions that are either incredibly glamorous and artistic or which involve being of service to others. The film industry is ruled by Pisces, and many members of your sign are photographers, actors, dancers, choreographers and designers. You're also attracted to the perfumery, cosmetics and fashion businesses. At the other extreme, many Pisceans devote their lives to looking after others, especially in institutions such as hospitals, prisons and religious orders.

Wherever you work, you need a sympathetic atmosphere, pleasant surroundings and colleagues who understand and appreciate you. Any job where you're nothing more than a drudge will quickly depress you and may eventually make you ill. You're one of the most creative signs of all, so ideally you should be able to express this side of your nature even if it's only in a small way. You also have a powerful imagination which needs a constructive outlet, otherwise it might play games with you.

MERCURY AND YOUR COMMUNICATIONS

Where would we be without Mercury? This tiny planet rules everything connected with our communications, from the way we speak to the way we get about. The position of Mercury in your birth chart describes how fast or how slow you absorb information, the sorts of things you talk about, the way you communicate with other people and how much nervous energy you have.

Mercury is an important part of everyone's birth chart, but it has extra meaning for Geminis and Virgos because both these signs are ruled by Mercury.

Mercury is the closest planet to the Sun in the solar system, and its orbit lies between the Earth and the Sun. In fact, it is never more than 28 degrees away from the Sun. Mercury is one of the smallest known planets in the solar system, but it makes up in speed what it lacks in size. It whizzes around the Sun at about 108,000 miles an hour, to avoid being sucked into the Sun's fiery mass.

If you've always wondered how astrology works, here's a brief explanation. Your horoscope (a map of the planets' positions at the time of your birth) is divided up into twelve sections, known as 'houses'. Each one represents a different area of your life, and together they cover every aspect of our experiences on Earth. As Mercury moves around the heavens each year it progresses through each house in turn, affecting a particular part of your life, such as your health or career. If you plot its progress through your own chart, you'll be able to make the most of Mercury's influence in 2000. That way, you'll know when it's best to make contact with others and when it's wisest to keep your thoughts to yourself.

Mercury takes just over one year to complete its orbit of the Earth, but during this time it doesn't always travel forwards, it also appears to go backwards. When this happens, it means that, from our vantage point on Earth, Mercury has slowed down to such an extent that it seems to be backtracking through the skies. We call this retrograde motion. When Mercury is travelling forwards, we call it direct motion.

All the planets, with the exception of the Sun and Moon, go retrograde at some point during their orbit of the Earth. A retrograde Mercury is very important because it means that during this time our communications can hit delays and snags. Messages may go missing, letters could get lost in the post, appliances and gadgets can go on the blink. You may also find it hard to make yourself understood. In 2000, there are several periods when Mercury goes retrograde. These are between 21 February and 14 March, 23 June and 17 July, and between 18 October and 8 November. These are all times to keep a close eye on your communications. You may also feel happiest if you can avoid signing important agreements or contracts during these times.

To plot the progress of Mercury, fill in the blank diagram on page 8, writing '1' in the section next to your Sun sign, then numbering consecutively in an anti-clockwise direction around the signs until you have completed them all. It will now be easy to chart Mercury's movements. When it is in the same sign as your Sun, Mercury is in your first house, when he moves into the next sign (assuming he's not going retrograde) he occupies your second house, and so on, until he reaches your twelfth house, at which point he will move back into your first house again.

Diagram 1

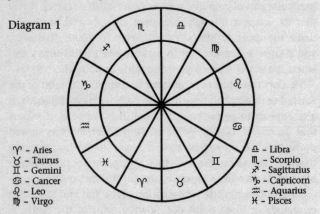

♈ – Aries
♉ – Taurus
♊ – Gemini
♋ – Cancer
♌ – Leo
♍ – Virgo

♎ – Libra
♏ – Scorpio
♐ – Sagittarius
♑ – Capricorn
♒ – Aquarius
♓ – Pisces

Here are the houses of the horoscope, numbered from one to twelve, for someone born with the Sun in Aquarius.

Diagram 2

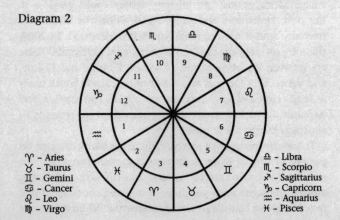

♈ – Aries
♉ – Taurus
♊ – Gemini
♋ – Cancer
♌ – Leo
♍ – Virgo

♎ – Libra
♏ – Scorpio
♐ – Sagittarius
♑ – Capricorn
♒ – Aquarius
♓ – Pisces

MERCURY'S ENTRY INTO THE SIGNS IN 2000
(All times are given in GMT, using the 24-hour clock)

January
Mercury is in Capricorn when 2000 begins

18	22:21	Aquarius

February

5	08:10	Pisces
21	12:47	Retrograde in Pisces

March

14	20:40	Direct in Pisces

April

13	00:18	Aries
30	03:54	Taurus

May

14	07:11	Gemini
30	04:28	Cancer

June

23	08:33	Retrograde in Cancer

July

17	13:21	Direct in Cancer

August

7	05:43	Leo
22	10:12	Virgo

September

7	21:23	Libra
28	13:29	Scorpio

October

18	13:42	Retrograde in Scorpio

November
7	07:29	Retrograde into Libra
8	02:29	Direct in Libra
8	21:43	Scorpio

December
3	20:27	Sagittarius
23	02:04	Capricorn

As 2000 begins, Mercury is moving through the final degrees of Capricorn, so it is in whichever house corresponds
with the sign of Capricorn in your diagram. For instance, if
you're an Aquarian, Mercury will move into your own sign
at 22:21 GMT on 18 January and will occupy your first
house. You can then read the explanation below telling you
what to expect at this time. Mercury next moves signs at
08:10 GMT on 5 February, when he moves into Pisces. So if
you're an Aquarian, Mercury will now be in your second
house.

Mercury in the First House

This is a very busy time for you and you're completely
wrapped up in your own ideas and concerns. Even if you
aren't usually very chatty, you certainly are at the moment.
However, you will much prefer talking about yourself to
listening to other people! You've got lots of nervous energy
at the moment and you'll enjoy getting out and about as
much as possible. Look for ways of burning off excess energy,
such as going for brisk walks or doing things that require
initiative. This is a great opportunity to think about ways of
pushing forward with ideas and getting new projects off the
ground.

Mercury in the Second House

This is a great time to think about things that mean a lot to you. These might be beliefs, philosophies or anything else that gives meaning to your life. It's also a good time to consider the people that make your world go round. Do you devote enough time to them? You should also spare a thought for your finances, because this is a perfect opportunity to scrutinize them and make sure everything is in order. You could get in touch with someone who can give you some financial advice, or you might do some research into how to put your money to good use.

Mercury in the Third House

Chatty? You bet! This is probably when you're at your most talkative, and you'll enjoy nattering away about whatever pops into your head. You'll love talking to whoever happens to be around, but you'll get on especially well with neighbours, people you see in the course of your daily routine and close relatives. You'll soon start to feel restless if you have to spend too long in one place, so grab every opportunity to vary your schedule. You'll love taking off on day trips, going away for weekend breaks or simply abandoning your usual routine and doing something completely different. Communications will go well and you'll love playing with gadgets and appliances.

Mercury in the Fourth House

Your thoughts are never far away from your home and family life at the moment. You may be thinking about ways of improving your living standards and you could talk to people who can give you some advice. You're also wrapped up in thoughts of the past, and you may even be assailed by memories of far-off events or things you haven't thought about in ages. Pay attention to your dreams because they could give you some invaluable insights into the way you're feeling. Watch out for a slight tendency to be defensive or to imagine that people are trying to get at you. It's a lovely time for getting in touch with your nearest and dearest who live a long way away.

Mercury in the Fifth House

You'll really enjoy putting your mind to good use at the moment, especially if you do things that are based on fun. For instance, you might get engrossed in competitions, jigsaw puzzles, crosswords and quizzes, especially if there's the chance of winning a prize! Children and pets will be terrific company and you'll love romping with them. However, you may find that they're a lot more playful than usual. You may even be on the receiving end of some practical jokes. It's a super time to go on holiday, particularly if you're visiting somewhere you've never been before. Your social life promises to keep you busy and you'll find it easy to talk to loved ones about things that matter to you.

Mercury in the Sixth House

This is the ideal time of year to think about your health and well-being. Are you looking after yourself properly? If you've been battling with some strange symptoms, this is the perfect opportunity to get them investigated so you can put your mind at rest. You'll enjoy reading about medical matters, such as immersing yourself in a book that tells you how to keep fit or extolling the virtues of a specific eating plan. Your work might also keep you busy. Colleagues and customers will be chatty, and you could spend a lot of time dealing with paperwork or tapping away on the computer. It's a great time to look for a new job, especially if that means scanning the newspaper adverts, joining an employment agency or writing lots of application letters.

Mercury in the Seventh House

Communications play an important role in all your relationships at the moment. This is your chance to put across your point of view and to keep other people posted about what you think. You may enjoy having lots of chats with partners or you might have something important to discuss. Either way, the key to success is to keep talking! You're prepared to reach a compromise, so it's a marvellous time to get involved in negotiations and discussions. You'll also find that two heads are better than one right now, so it's the ideal time to do some teamwork. You'll enjoy bouncing your ideas off other people and listening to what they have to say.

Mercury in the Eighth House

It's time to turn your attention to your shared resources and official money matters. So if you share a bank account with your partner, you should check that everything is running smoothly. You might even decide to open a new account that suits you better or that pays a higher rate of interest. Speaking of accounts, this is an excellent time to fill in your tax return or complete your accounts for the year because you're in the right frame of mind for such things. This is also a good time to think about your close relationships. Do they bring you the emotional satisfaction that you need or is something missing? If you think there's room for improvement, talk to your partner about how to make things better between you.

Mercury in the Ninth House

The more you can expand your mental and physical horizons now, the happier you'll be. It's a time of year when you're filled with intellectual curiosity about the world and you long to cram your head with all sorts of facts and figures. You might decide to do some studying, whether you do it on a very informal basis or enrol for an evening class or college course. You'll certainly enjoy browsing around bookshops and library shelves, looking for books on your favourite subjects. Travel will appeal to you too, especially if you can visit somewhere exotic or a place that you've never been to before. You might become interested in a different religion from your own or you could be engrossed in something connected with philosophy, history or spirituality.

Mercury in the Tenth House

Spend some time thinking about your career prospects. Are you happy with the way things are going or does your professional life need a rethink? This is a great opportunity to talk to people who can give you some good advice. It's also an excellent time to share your ideas with your boss or a superior, especially if you're hoping to impress them. You could hear about a promotion or some improved job prospects, or you might decide to apply for a completely new job. It's also a marvellous opportunity to increase your qualifications, perhaps by training for something new or brushing up on an existing skill. You'll find it easier than usual to talk to older friends and relatives, especially if they can sometimes be a little tricky or hard to please.

Mercury in the Eleventh House

This is a great time to enjoy the company of friends and acquaintances. You'll love talking to them, especially if you can chat about subjects that make you think or that have humanitarian overtones. All sorts of intellectual activities will appeal to you at the moment. If your social circle is getting smaller and smaller, grab this chance to widen your horizons by meeting people who are on the same wavelength as you. For instance, you might decide to join a new club or society that caters for one of your interests. It's also a good opportunity to think about your hopes and wishes for the future. Are they going according to plan, or should you revise your strategy or even start again from scratch?

Mercury in the Twelfth House

You're entering a very reflective and reclusive period when you want to retreat from the madding crowd and have some time to yourself. You might enjoy taking the phone off the hook and curling up with a good book, or you could spend time studying subjects by yourself. There will be times when you feel quite tongue-tied, and you'll find it difficult to say exactly what you mean. You may even want to maintain a discreet silence on certain subjects, but make sure that other people don't take advantage of this by putting words into your mouth. You could be the recipient of someone's confidences, in which case you'll be a sympathetic listener. If you want to tell someone your secrets, choose your confidante wisely.

LOVE AND THE STARS

Love makes the world go round. When we know we're loved, we walk on air. We feel confident, happy and joyous. Without love, we feel miserable, lonely and as if life isn't worth living. If you're still looking for your perfect partner, this is the ideal guide for you. It will tell you which Sun signs you get on best with and which ones aren't such easy-going mates. By the way, there is hope for every astrological combination, and none are out and out disasters. It's simply that you'll find it easier to get on well with some signs than with others.

At the end of this section you'll see two compatibility charts – one showing how you get on in the love and sex stakes, and the other one telling you which signs make the best friends. These charts will instantly remind you which signs get on best and which struggle to keep the peace. Each combination has been given marks out of ten, with ten points being a fabulous pairing and one point being pretty grim. Find the woman's Sun sign along the top line of the chart, then look down the left-hand column for the man's sign. The square where these two lines meet will give you the result of this astrological combination. For instance, when assessing the love and sex compatibility of a Leo woman and a Cancerian man, they score six out of ten.

 **Pisces**

Relationships mean a lot to a sensitive Piscean, but they're easily misunderstood by many of the more robust signs. There are no such worries with the other Water signs, however. A Piscean loves being with a tender Cancerian who knows how to help them relax and feel safe. They really enjoy playing house together but the emotional scenes will blow the roof off. The relationship between a Piscean and a Scorpio can be quite spicy and sexy, but the Piscean is turned off if the Scorpio becomes too intense and dramatic. Two Pisceans feel safe with one another, but they'll push all their problems under the carpet unless one of them is more objective.

A Piscean also gets on well with the Earth signs, although with a few reservations. A Piscean takes comfort from being looked after by a protective Taurean, but after a while they could feel stifled by the Taurean's possessive and matter-of-fact attitude. The relationship between a Piscean and a Virgo starts off well but the Piscean could soon feel crushed by the Virgo's criticism and will need more emotional reassurance than the Virgo is able to give. A Piscean feels safe with a Capricorn because they're so dependable but in the end this may begin to bug them. It's not that they want the Capricorn to two-time them, more that they'd like a little unpredictability every now and then.

A Piscean is fascinated by the Air signs but their apparent lack of emotion could cause problems. A Piscean and a Gemini are terrific friends but could encounter difficulties as lovers. The Piscean's strong emotional needs are too much for the Gemini to handle – they'll feel as if they're drowning. The Piscean is on much firmer ground with a Libran, who'll go out of their way to keep the Piscean happy. Neither sign is good at facing up to any nasty truths, however. An Aquarian is too much for a sensitive Piscean, who views the world through rose-coloured specs. An Aquarian, on the other hand, has uncomfortably clear vision.

The Fire signs can cheer up a Piscean enormously, but any prolonged displays of emotion will make the Fire signs feel weighed down. The Piscean is fascinated by an Arien's exploits but could feel reluctant to join in. They'll also be easily hurt by some of the Arien's off-the-cuff remarks. When a Piscean pairs up with a Leo they appreciate the way the Leo wants to take charge and look after them. After a while, however, this could grate on them and they'll want to be more independent. A Piscean enjoys discussing philosophy and spiritual ideas with a Sagittarian – they can sit up half the night talking things through. The Sagittarian brand of honesty could hurt the Piscean at times, but they know this isn't malicious and will quickly forgive such outbursts.

 Aries

Because Ariens belong to the Fire element, they get on very well with their fellow Fire signs Leo and Sagittarius. All the same, an Arien getting together with a Leo will soon notice a distinct drop in their bank balance, because they'll enjoy going to all the swankiest restaurants and sitting in the best seats at the theatre. When an Arien pairs up with a Sagittarian, they'll compete over who drives the fastest car and has the most exciting holidays. When two Ariens get together the results can be combustible. Ideally, one Arien should be a lot quieter, otherwise they'll spend most of their time jostling for power. All these combinations are very sexy and physical.

Ariens also thrive in the company of the three Air signs – Gemini, Libra and Aquarius. Of the three, they get on best with Geminis, who share their rather childlike view of the world and also their sense of fun. An Arien and a Gemini enjoy hatching all sorts of ideas and schemes, even if they never get round to putting them into action. There's an exciting sense of friction between Aries and Libra, their opposite number in the zodiac. An Arien will be enchanted by the way their Libran caters to their every need, but may become impatient when the Libran also wants to look after other people. An Arien will be captivated by the originality of an Aquarian, although at times they'll be driven mad by the Aquarian's eccentric approach to life and the way they blow hot and cold in the bedroom.

Ariens don't do so well with the Earth signs – Taurus, Virgo and Capricorn. The very careful, slightly plodding nature of a typical Taurean can drive an Arien barmy at times, and although they'll respect – and benefit from – the Taurean's practical approach to life, it can still fill them with irritation. An Arien finds it difficult to fathom a Virgo, because their attitudes to life are diametrically opposed. An Arien likes to jump in with both feet, while a Virgo prefers to take things slowly and analyse every possibility before committing themselves. An Arien can get on quite well with a Capricorn, because they're linked by their sense of ambition and their earthy sexual needs.

An Arien is out of their depth with any of the Water signs – Cancer, Scorpio and Pisces. They quickly become irritated by the defensive Cancerian, although they'll love their cooking. An Arien will enjoy a very passionate affair with a Scorpio, but the Scorpio's need to know exactly what the Arien is up to when their back is turned will soon cause problems and rifts. Although an Arien may begin a relationship with a Pisces by wanting to look after them and protect them from the harsh realities of life, eventually the Piscean's extremely sensitive nature may bring out the Arien's bullying streak.

 **Taurus**

Taureans are literally in their element when they're with Virgos or Capricorns who, like themselves, are Earth signs. Two Taureans will get along very happily together, although they could become so wedded to routine that they get stuck in a rut. They may also encourage one another to eat too much. A Taurean will enjoy being with a Virgo, because they respect the Virgo's methodical nature. They'll also like encouraging their Virgo to relax and take life easy. Money will form a link between a Taurean and a Capricorn, with plenty of serious discussions on how to make it and what to do with it once they've got it. There will also be a strong sexual rapport, and the Taurean will encourage the more sensual side of the Capricorn.

The relationship between a Taurean and members of the Water element is also very good. A Taurean and a Cancerian will revel in one another's company and will probably be so happy at home that they'll rarely stir from their armchairs. They both have a strong need for emotional security and will stick together through thick and thin. There's plenty of passion when a Taurean pairs up with a Scorpio, although the faithful Taurean could become fed up with the Scorpio's jealous nature. They simply won't understand what they're being accused of, and their loyal nature will be offended by the very thought that they could be a two-timer. A Taurean will be delighted by a delicate Piscean, and will want to take care of such a vulnerable and sensitive creature.

Things become rather more complicated when a Taurean pairs up with an Arien, Leo or Sagittarian, all of whom are Fire signs. They have very little in common – Taureans like to take things slowly while Fire signs want to make things happen *now*. It's particularly difficult between a Taurean and an Arien – the careful Taurean will feel harried and rushed by the impetuous Arien. It's a little better when a Taurean gets together with a Leo, because they share a deep appreciation of the good things in life, although the Taurean will be horrified by the Leo's ability to spend money. Making joint decisions could be difficult, however, because they'll both stand their ground and refuse to budge. A Taurean and a Sagittarian simply don't understand each other – they're on such different wavelengths. Any Taurean displays of possessiveness will make the independent Sagittarian want to run a mile.

Taureans are equally mystified by the Air signs – Gemini, Libra and Aquarius. What they see as the flightiness of Gemini drives them barmy – why can't the Gemini settle down and do one thing at a time? The Taurean will probably feel quite exhausted by the Gemini's many interests and bubbly character. Taurus and Libra are a surprisingly good pairing, because they share a need for beauty, luxury and love. This could end up costing the penny-wise Taurean quite a packet, but they'll have a deliciously romantic time along the way. Taurus and Aquarius are chalk and cheese, and neither one is prepared to meet the other one halfway. The Taurean need to keep tabs on their loved one's every movement will irritate the freedom-loving Aquarian, and there will be plenty of rows as a result.

♊ Gemini

One of the Air signs, Geminis get on very well with their fellow members of this element – Librans and Aquarians. Two Geminis are the astrological equivalent of double trouble – they chat nineteen to the dozen and revel in the company of someone who understands them so well. A Gemini delights in being with a Libran, because they enjoy the intellectual company and will benefit from the Libran's (usually) relaxed approach to life. They'll also learn to deal with their emotions more if a sympathetic Libran can guide them. Gemini and Aquarius is a very exciting pairing – the Gemini is encouraged to think deeply and knows that the Aquarian won't put up with any woolly ideas or fudged arguments.

Geminis also get on well with the three Fire signs – Aries, Leo and Sagittarius. A Gemini loves being with a racy, adventurous Arien, and together they enjoy keeping abreast of all the latest gossip and cultural developments. However, after the first flush of enthusiasm has worn off, the Gemini may find the Arien's strong need for sex rather hard to take. The Gemini gets on very well with a Leo. They delight in the Leo's affectionate nature and are amused by their need to have the best that money can buy – and they'll gladly share in the spoils. Gemini and Sagittarius are an excellent combination, because they sit opposite each other in the zodiac and so complement one another's character. The Gemini will be fascinated by the erudite and knowledgeable Sagittarian.

Gemini doesn't do so well with the Earth signs of Taurus and Capricorn, although they get on better with Virgo. The Gemini finds it difficult to understand a Taurean, because they see the world from such different viewpoints. The Gemini takes a more light-hearted approach and lives life at such a speed that they find it difficult to slow down to the more measured pace of a Taurean. The wonderfully dry Capricorn sense of humour is a source of constant delight to a Gemini. However, they're less taken with the Capricorn's streak of pessimism and their love of tradition. Of the three Earth signs, Gemini and Virgo are the most compatible. The Gemini shares the Virgo's brainpower and they have long, fascinating conversations.

When a Gemini gets together with the Water signs, the result can be enjoyable or puzzling. Gemini and Cancer have little in common, because the Gemini wants to spread their emotional and intellectual wings, whereas a Cancerian likes to stay close to home and has little interest in abstract ideas. Gemini finds

Scorpio perplexing because they operate on such different levels. A Gemini tends to skim along the surface of things, so often deals with life on a superficial level, whereas a Scorpio likes to dig deep and has to have an emotional investment in everything they do. A Gemini appreciates the subtlety and sensitivity of a Piscean, but they're likely to make off-the-cuff comments that unwittingly hurt the Piscean.

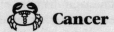 **Cancer**

Cancerians revel in the company of their fellow Water signs of Scorpio and Pisces. When two Cancerians get together they could spend most of their time at home or eating – preferably both. They feel safe in the knowledge that they both have a strong need for love, but their innate Cancerian tenacity may mean they cling on to the relationship even if it's long past its best. A Cancerian is enchanted with a Scorpio, because at last they feel free to really let rip emotionally. However, the intuitive Cancerian should beware of soaking up the Scorpio's darker moods like a psychic sponge. A Cancerian will take one look at a delicate Piscean and want to invite them home for a good hot meal. All the Cancerian's protective instincts are aroused by a gentle Piscean, but their anger will also be aroused if it turns out the Piscean has been leading a double life behind their back.

Cancerians also find a great deal of comfort in the company of the Earth signs – Taurus, Virgo and Capricorn. Cancer and Taurus were made for each other – they both adore home comforts and they trust one another implicitly. The Cancerian loves making a cosy nest for their hard-working Taurean. A Cancerian finds a Virgo a more difficult proposition, especially emotionally. Whereas Cancer is all warm hugs and holding hands by the fire, Virgo prefers to read a book and reserve any displays of affection for the bedroom. Cancer and Capricorn are opposite numbers in the zodiac, so share a tremendous rapport. They also share the same values of home, tradition and family, and if anyone can help a Capricorn to relax and take life easy, it's a Cancerian.

Life becomes more difficult when it comes to a Cancerian's relationship with any of the Air signs. They simply don't understand one another. A Cancerian can't make a Gemini out. They feel confused by what they think of as the Gemini's flightiness and inability to stay in one place for long. They can also be easily hurt by the Gemini's difficulty in expressing their emotions. A Cancerian gets on much better with a Libran. They're both ambitious in their own ways and so have a great deal in common. The Cancerian enjoys the Libran's romantic nature, but the Cancerian tendency to cling doesn't go down well. A Cancerian regards a typical Aquarian as a being from another planet. They're hurt by the Aquarian's strong need for independence and dislike of having to account for their every action, and are dismayed and confused by the Aquarian's hot-and-cold attitude to sex.

The Fire signs of Aries, Leo and Sagittarius are also a potential source of bewilderment to the gentle Cancerian. They understand the drive and ambition of an Arien, but will be stung by their blunt speech and worried about their daredevil tendencies. What if they hurt themselves? A Cancerian gets on well with a Leo because they share a strong love of family and are both openly affectionate and loving. The Cancerian enjoys creating a home that the Leo can feel proud of. So far, so good, but the story isn't so simple when a Cancerian pairs up with a Sagittarian. They're too different to understand one another – the Cancerian wants to stay at home with the family while the Sagittarian has an instinctive need to roam the world. As a result, the Cancerian will be disappointed, and then hurt, when the Sagittarian's busy schedule takes them away from home too often.

Leo

Leos adore the company of their fellow Fire signs, Ariens and Sagittarius. They understand one another and enjoy each other's spontaneous warmth and affection. A Leo is amused by the exuberance and impulsiveness of an Arien, and they enjoy being persuaded to let their hair down a bit and not worry too much about appearances. A Leo enjoys the dash and vitality of a Sagittarian, although they may feel irritated if they can never get hold of them on the phone or the Sagittarian is always off doing other things. Two Leos together either love or loathe one another. One of them should be prepared to take a back seat, otherwise they'll both be vying for the limelight all the time.

The three Air signs of Gemini, Libra and Aquarius all get on well with Leos. When a Leo pairs up with a Gemini, you can expect lots of laughter and plenty of fascinating conversations. The demonstrative Leo is able to help the Gemini be more openly affectionate and loving. Leo and Libra is a great combination, and the Leo is enchanted by the Libran's fair-minded attitude. Both signs love luxury and all the good things in life but their bank managers may not be so pleased by the amount of the money they manage to spend. Leo and Aquarius sit opposite one another across the horoscope, so they already have a great deal in common. They're fascinated by one another but they're both very stubborn, so any disputes between them usually end in stalemate because neither is prepared to concede any ground.

Leos don't really understand the Earth signs. Although Leos admire their practical approach to life, they find it rather restricting. A Leo enjoys the sensuous and hedonistic side of a Taurean's character but may become frustrated by their fear of change. Leo and Virgo have very little in common, especially when it comes to food – the Leo wants to tuck in at all the best restaurants while the Virgo is worried about the state of the kitchens, the number of calories and the size of the bill. A Leo respects the Capricorn's desire to support their family and approves of their need to be seen in the best possible light, but they feel hurt by the Capricorn's difficulty in showing their feelings.

When a Leo gets together with one of the Water signs – Cancer, Scorpio or Pisces – they'll enjoy the sexual side of the relationship but could eventually feel stifled by all that Watery emotion. A Leo and a Cancerian adore making a home together and both dote on their children. The Leo also likes comforting their vulnerable Cancerian – provided this doesn't happen too often. A Leo and a Scorpio will be powerfully attracted to one another, but power could also pull them apart – who's going to wear the trousers? They'll also lock horns during rows and both of them will refuse to back down. A Leo delights in a sophisticated Piscean, but may become irritated by their indecision and jangly nerves.

 **Virgo**

As you might imagine, Virgos are happy with their fellow Earth signs of Taurus and Capricorn because they share the same practical attitude. A Virgo enjoys the steady, reassuring company of a Taurean, and they might even learn to relax a little instead of worrying themselves into the ground over the slightest problem. When two Virgos get together it can be too much of a good thing. Although at first they'll love talking to someone who shares so many of their preoccupations and ideas, they can soon drive one another round the bend. When a Virgo first meets a Capricorn they're delighted to know someone who's obviously got their head screwed on. It's only later on that they wish the Capricorn could lighten up every now and then.

Virgos get on well with Cancerians, Scorpios and Pisceans, the three Water signs. A Virgo enjoys being looked after by a considerate Cancerian, although they'll worry about their waistline and may get irritated by the Cancerian's super-sensitive feelings. You can expect plenty of long, analytical conversations when a Virgo gets together with a Scorpio. They both love getting to the bottom of subjects and will endlessly talk things through. They'll also get on extremely well in the bedroom. Pisces is Virgo's opposite sign, but although some opposites thrive in each other's company, that isn't always the case with this combination. The Virgo could soon grow im-patient with the dreamy Piscean and will long to tell them a few home truths.

Although the other Earth signs don't usually get on well with Air signs, it's different for Virgos. They understand the intellectual energies of Geminis, Librans and Aquarians. A Virgo thrives in a Gemini's company, and they spend hours chatting over the phone if they can't get together in person. It's difficult for them to discuss their emotions, however, and they may never tell each other how they really feel. A Virgo admires a sophisticated, charming Libran, and marvels at their diplomacy. How do they do it? Expect a few sparks to fly when a Virgo pairs up with an Aquarian, because both of them have very strong opinions and aren't afraid to air them. The result is a lot of hot air and some vigorous arguments.

The three Fire signs – Aries, Leo and Sagittarius – are a source of endless fascination to a Virgo. They've got so much energy! A Virgo finds an Arien exciting but their relationship could be short-lived because the Virgo will be so irritated by the Arien's devil-may-care attitude to life. When a Virgo pairs up with a Leo, they'll be intrigued by this person's comparatively lavish lifestyle but their own modest temperament will be shocked if the Leo enjoys showing off. A Virgo is able to talk to a Sagittarius until the cows come home – they're both fascinated by ideas, although the precise Virgo will first be amused, and then irritated, by the Sagittarian's rather relaxed attitude to hard facts.

♎ Libra

Of all the members of the zodiac, this is the one that finds it easiest to get on with the other signs. Librans get on particularly well with Geminis and Aquarians, their fellow Air signs. A Libran is enchanted by a Gemini's quick brain and ready wit, and they enjoy endless discussions on all sorts of subjects. When two Librans get together, they revel in the resulting harmonious atmosphere but it's almost impossible for them to reach any decisions – each one defers to the other while being unable to say what they really want. A Libran is intrigued by the independence and sharp mind of an Aquarian, but their feelings could be hurt by the Aquarian's emotional coolness.

Libra enjoys being with the three Fire signs – Aries, Leo and Sagittarius. Libra, who often takes life at rather a slow pace, is energized by a lively Arien, and they complement one another's personalities well. However, the Libran may occasionally feel hurt by the Arien's single-mindedness and blunt speech. A Libran adores the luxury-loving ways of a Leo, and they'll both spend a fortune in the pursuit of happiness. They also get on well in the bedroom. When a Libran gets together with an exuberant Sagittarian, they'll have great fun. All the same, the Sagittarian need for honesty could fluster the Libran, who adopts a much more diplomatic approach to life.

Although the other two Air signs can find it hard to understand members of the Water element, it's different for Librans. They're more sympathetic to the emotional energies of Cancerians, Scorpios and Pisceans. A Libran delights in the protective care of a Cancerian, but those ever-changing Cancerians moods may be hard for a balanced Libran to take.

Those deep Scorpio emotions will intrigue the Libran but they may quickly become bogged down by such an intense outlook on life and will be desperate for some light relief. As for Pisces, the Libran is charmed by the Piscean's delicate nature and creative gifts, but both signs hate facing up to unpleasant facts so this couple may never deal with any problems that lie between them.

Libra enjoys the reliable natures of Taurus, Virgo and Capricorn, the Earth signs. A Libran appreciates the company of a relaxed and easy-going Taurean, although they may sometimes regret the Taurean's lack of imagination. When a Libran and a Virgo get together, the Libran enjoys the Virgo's mental abilities but their critical comments will soon cut the Libran to the quick. The Libran may not come back for a second tongue-lashing. A Libran understands the ambitions of a Capricorn, and likes their steady nature and the way they support their family. However, there could soon be rows about money, with the Libran spending a lot more than the Capricorn thinks is necessary.

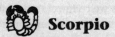 **Scorpio**

Not every sign gets on well with its fellow members, yet an astonishing number of Scorpios pair up. They feel safe together because they know the worst and best about each other. When things are good, they're brilliant but these two can also bring out the worst in each other, with intense silences and brooding sulks. A Scorpio enjoys the tender ministrations of a loving Cancerian, and adores being with someone who's so obviously concerned about their welfare. Feelings run deep when a Scorpio pairs up with a Piscean, although the Scorpio may become impatient with the Piscean's reluctance to face up to unpalatable truths.

The three Earth signs, Taurus, Virgo and Capricorn, are well-suited to the Scorpio temperament. Those astrological opposites, Scorpio and Taurus, enjoy a powerful relationship, much of which probably takes place in the bedroom, but whenever they have a disagreement there's an atmosphere you could cut with a knife, and neither of them will be prepared to admit they were in the wrong. A Scorpio is attracted to a neat, analytical Virgo but their feelings will be hurt by this sign's tendency to criticize. What's more, their pride stops them telling the Virgo how they feel. The Scorpio admires a practical Capricorn, especially if they've earned a lot of respect through their work, but this could be a rather chilly pairing because both signs find it difficult to show their feelings.

When you put a Scorpio together with one of the three Fire signs, they'll either get on famously or won't understand one another at all. A Scorpio revels in the lusty Arien's sex drive, although they'll soon feel tired if they try to keep up with the Arien's busy schedule. The combination of Scorpio and Leo packs quite a punch. They're both very strong personalities, but they boss one another around like mad and find it almost impossible to achieve a compromise if they fall out. A Scorpio likes to take life at a measured pace, so they're bemused by a Sagittarian's need to keep busy all the time. In the end, they'll become fed up with never seeing the Sagittarian, or playing second fiddle to all their other interests.

Scorpio is bemused by the three Air signs – Gemini, Libran and Aquarius – because they operate on such completely different wavelengths. A Scorpio can be good friends with a Gemini but they're at emotional cross-purposes, with the Scorpio's intense approach to life too much for a light-hearted Gemini to cope with. Emotions are also the bugbear between a Scorpio and a Libran. Everything is great at first, but the Scorpio's powerful feelings and dark moods will eventually send the Libran running in the opposite direction. You can expect some tense arguments when a Scorpio pairs up with an Aquarian – they're both convinced that they're right and the other one is wrong.

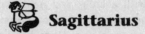 **Sagittarius**

When a Sagittarian pairs up with a fellow Fire sign, there's plenty of warmth and the odd firework. A Sagittarian is thrilled by the adventurous spirit of an Arien, and they love exploring the world together. There are plenty of tall tales when a Sagittarian gets together with a Leo – they'll try to outdo each other, dropping names and recounting their greatest triumphs. If the Leo is slightly pompous, the Sagittarian is able to take them down a peg or two, but they must beware of hurting the Leo's feelings. As for two Sagittarians, they'll spur each other on and encourage one another to gain as much experience of life as possible. You probably won't be able to move in their house for books.

With their endless curiosity about the world, Sagittarians understand the intellectual Air signs very well. A Sagittarian enjoys the chatty company of a Gemini and, because they're opposite numbers in the zodiac, the Sagittarian is able to encourage the Gemini to see things through and explore them in more detail than usual. A refined and diplomatic Libran will try to teach the blunt Sagittarian not to say the first thing that pops into their head. However, the Sagittarian may eventually find the Libran's sense of balance rather trying – why can't they get more worked up about things? There's plenty of straight talking when a Sagittarian teams up with an Aquarian – they both have a high regard for honesty. The independent Sagittarian respects the Aquarian's need for freedom, but may feel rather stung by their periods of emotional coolness.

A Sagittarian will struggle to understand the Earth signs.

They respect the Taurean's ability to work hard but they're driven to distraction by their reluctance to make changes and break out of any ruts they've fallen into. A Sagittarian enjoys talking to a brainy Virgo, but their expansive and spontaneous nature could eventually be restricted by the Virgo's need to think things through before taking action. When a Sagittarian gets together with a Capricorn, it's a case of optimism versus pessimism. While the Sagittarian's glass is half-full, the Capricorn's is always half-empty, and this causes many rows and possibly some ill feeling.

There could be lots of misunderstandings when a Sagittarian gets involved with one of the Water signs. A Sagittarian needs a bigger social circle than their family, whereas a Cancerian is quite happy surrounded by kith and kin. The Sagittarian need for independence won't go down well, either. It's like oil and water when a Sagittarian pairs up with a Scorpio. The Sagittarian is the roamer of the zodiac, whereas the Scorpio wants them where they can see them, in case they're up to no good. All will be well if the Sagittarian gets together with a strong-minded Piscean. In fact, they'll really enjoy one another's company. A Piscean who's lost in a world of their own, however, will soon leave them cold.

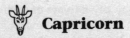 **Capricorn**

Despite their outward poise, a Capricorn is very easily hurt so they need to know their feelings won't be trampled on. There's least danger of that when they get together with a fellow Earth sign. A Capricorn adores a Taurean's deep sense of responsibility and they'll both work hard to create their ideal home. A Capricorn appreciates the methodical approach of a Virgo, but could feel deeply hurt by the Virgo's sharp tongue and caustic remarks. If two Capricorns team up, one of them must be demonstrative and openly affectionate, otherwise the relationship could be rather sterile and serious.

Capricorns also feel safe with members of the Water signs. When a Capricorn gets together with a Cancerian, they do their utmost to make their home a haven. They'll get great satisfaction from channelling their energies into bringing up a family. A Capricorn may be rather bemused by the depth and intensity of a Scorpio's emotions – Capricorns are too reserved to indulge in such drama themselves and it can make them feel uncomfortable. A no-nonsense Capricorn could be perplexed by an extremely vulnerable Piscean and won't know how to handle them. Should they give them a hanky or tell them to pull themselves together?

The Air signs can also make a Capricorn feel somewhat unsettled. They're fascinated by a Gemini's breadth of knowledge and endless chat, but they also find them superficial and rather flighty. In fact, the Capricorn probably doesn't trust the Gemini. A Capricorn feels far happier in the company of a Libran. Here's someone who seems much steadier emotionally and who can help the Capricorn to unwind after a hard day's work. It can be great or ghastly when a Capricorn sets their sights on an Aquarian. They understand each other provided the Aquarian isn't too unconventional, but the Capricorn feels uncomfortable and embarrassed by any displays of eccentricity, deliberate or not.

The Fire signs help to warm up the Capricorn, who can be rather remote and distant at times. A Capricorn admires the Arien's drive and initiative, but endlessly tells them to look before they leap and could become irritated when they don't take this sage advice. When a Capricorn gets together with a Leo, they won't need to worry about appearances – the Capricorn will feel justly proud of the smart Leo. However, they could wince when the bills come in and they discover how much those clothes cost. A Capricorn thinks a Sagittarian must have come from another planet – how can they be so relaxed and laid-back all the time? They have great respect for the Sagittarian's wisdom and philosophy, but they quickly become fed up with having to fit in around the Sagittarian's hectic social life.

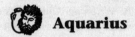

Aquarius

Put an Aquarian with a fellow Air sign and they're happy. They thoroughly enjoy being with a lively Gemini and love discussing everything under the sun with them. They may not have a very exciting sex life, but their mental closeness will more than make up for it. The gentle charms of a Libran calms down an Aquarian when their nerves become frayed, although they disapprove of the Libran's innate tact and diplomacy – why can't they just say what they think, instead of sitting on the fence? With two Aquarians you never know what to expect, other than that they'll be great friends. They'll certainly do a lot of talking, but could spend more time debating esoteric ideas and abstract concepts.

An Aquarian likes all the Fire signs, although they find Ariens hard to fathom and can become exhausted by an Arien's endless supply of energy and enthusiasm. There are no such problems when an Aquarian pairs up with a Leo because they complement each other in many ways. The Aquarian teaches objectivity to the Leo, who in return encourages the Aquarian to express their emotions more. An Aquarian thoroughly enjoys being with a Sagittarian because both of them hate being tied down. As a result, they respect one another's independence and will probably rarely see each other because of all their spare-time activities.

It's not quite so simple when an Aquarian joins forces

with one of the Earth signs. An Aquarian will lock horns with a Taurean sooner or later, because neither of them is able to back down once a disagreement has started. The Aquarian will also feel very restricted by the Taurean's possessiveness. The Virgo's analytical approach to life intrigues the Aquarian but they'll sit up all night arguing the toss over everything, with each one convinced that they've got all the answers. When an Aquarian meets a Capricorn, they've got their work cut out for them if they're to find a happy medium between the erratic Aquarian and the conventional Capricorn.

An Aquarian feels out of their depth when they're with one of the Water signs. They simply don't understand what makes a Cancerian tick – why do they worry themselves sick over things that they can't change? The Aquarian finds it all most peculiar. They also find it difficult to understand a Scorpio who takes so many things so seriously. Although the Aquarian also has a list of topics that mean a lot to them, they're not the sort of things that hold the slightest interest for a Scorpio. It's more or less the same story with a Pisces, because their huge resources of emotion make the Aquarian feel uncomfortable and fill them with a strong desire to escape as fast as possible.

Compatibility in Love and Sex at a glance

F M	♈	♉	♊	♋	♌	♍	♎	♏	♐	♑	♒	♓
♈	8	5	9	7	9	4	7	8	9	7	7	3
♉	6	8	4	10	7	8	8	7	3	8	2	8
♊	8	2	7	3	8	7	9	4	9	4	9	4
♋	5	10	4	8	6	5	6	8	2	9	2	8
♌	9	8	9	7	7	4	9	6	8	7	9	6
♍	4	8	6	4	4	7	6	7	7	9	4	4
♎	7	8	10	7	8	5	9	6	9	6	10	6
♏	7	9	4	7	6	6	7	10	5	6	5	7
♐	9	4	10	4	9	7	8	4	9	6	9	5
♑	7	8	4	9	6	8	6	4	4	8	4	5
♒	8	6	9	4	9	4	9	6	8	7	8	2
♓	7	6	7	9	6	7	6	9	7	5	4	9

1 = the pits
10 = the peaks

Key

♈ – Aries
♉ – Taurus
♊ – Gemini
♋ – Cancer
♌ – Leo
♍ – Virgo

♎ – Libra
♏ – Scorpio
♐ – Sagittarius
♑ – Capricorn
♒ – Aquarius
♓ – Pisces

Compatibility in Friendship at a glance

M\F	♈	♉	♊	♋	♌	♍	♎	♏	♐	♑	♒	♓
♈	8	5	10	5	9	3	7	8	9	6	8	5
♉	6	9	6	10	7	8	7	6	4	9	3	9
♊	9	3	9	4	9	8	10	5	10	5	10	6
♋	6	9	4	9	5	4	6	9	4	10	3	9
♌	10	7	9	6	9	4	8	6	9	6	9	7
♍	5	9	8	4	4	8	5	8	8	10	5	6
♎	8	9	10	8	8	6	9	5	9	6	10	7
♏	7	8	5	8	7	7	6	9	4	5	6	8
♐	9	5	10	4	10	8	8	4	10	7	9	6
♑	6	9	5	10	6	9	5	5	4	9	5	6
♒	9	6	10	5	9	5	9	7	9	5	9	3
♓	6	7	6	10	6	8	8	7	9	8	6	4	10

1 = the pits
10 = the peaks

Key

♈ – Aries
♉ – Taurus
♊ – Gemini
♋ – Cancer
♌ – Leo
♍ – Virgo

♎ – Libra
♏ – Scorpio
♐ – Sagittarius
♑ – Capricorn
♒ – Aquarius
♓ – Pisces

HOBBIES AND THE STARS

What do you do in your spare time? If you're looking for some new interests to keep you occupied in 2000, read on to discover which hobbies are ideal for your Sun sign.

 Pisces

Anything artistic or creative is perfect for you, because you have abundant gifts at your disposal. Painting, drawing, writing poetry and dancing are all classic Piscean pastimes. In fact, you may feel rather fed up or stifled when you can't express yourself creatively. When you want to escape from the world, you love going to the cinema or the theatre. You're a Water sign so you enjoy any activities connected with water, such as swimming or other forms of water sports. Many Pisceans enjoy gardening, and you'll especially like having some form of water feature in your garden even if it's very modest. You're very musical, and would enjoy learning to play an instrument if you can't already do so. You might also like using your psychic talents, perhaps by learning to read the tarot or runes.

Aries

Ariens love to keep active, so you aren't interested in any sort of hobby that's very sedentary or that keeps you glued to the sofa. You much prefer being kept busy, especially if it's out of doors. You also have a strong sense of adventure and a great love of speed, so one hobby that's right up your street is motor-racing. You might be lucky enough to be the driver, or you could be a spectator shouting yourself hoarse from the stands, but this is a sport you love. Speaking of sports, anything that's competitive and which threatens to knock the stuffing out of you will also suit you down to the ground. Rugby, football and baseball all fit the bill, and you might also enjoy martial arts and Eastern forms of exercise such as T'ai Chi.

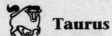

Taurus

You belong to one of the Earth signs, so it's no surprise that many Taureans were born with green fingers. You always feel better when you can be out in the fresh air, especially if you're in beautiful surroundings, so you adore gardening. Even if you're not keen on wielding a spade yourself you'll enjoy appreciating other people's efforts. Cooking is something that has enormous appeal for you and you enjoy creating gourmet meals, especially if the ingredients include your favourite foods. You also enjoy visiting swanky restaurants, although some of the gilt will be wiped off the gingerbread if you don't think you're getting value for money. Members of your sign are renowned for having beautiful voices so you might enjoy singing in a choir or on your own.

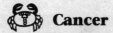

Gemini

One of your favourite ways of passing the time is to curl up with a good book. You'll eagerly read newspapers and magazines as well, and you always attempt crosswords and other sorts of puzzle even if you don't always finish them. Jigsaws intrigue you, especially if you can do something else at the same time, such as listening to music or watching the TV. You belong to a sign that doesn't like sitting still for long and you absolutely thrive on keeping active, so it's important for you to enjoy hobbies that make sure you get plenty of exercise. Tennis is a classic Gemini sport because it involves a lot of skill but it also boosts your social life. Dancing is another activity that helps you to keep fit while having a really good time.

Cancer

Home comforts are very important to you, so you spend a lot of time and money on making sure your home is the way you want it. You may enjoy reading magazines on interior design or you could be glued to all the DIY programmes on TV, adapting the best ideas for your own home. One of your greatest skills is cooking, because you belong to a sign that derives enormous emotional comfort from food. You take pleasure in cooking for your loved ones and you probably have a big collection of cookery books to provide you with endless inspiration. Water sports could appeal to you, especially if they involve visiting your favourite beach. You might also enjoy fishing, particularly if you can do it by moonlight.

Leo

You have a host of artistic skills and talents at your fingertips because you belong to the one of the most creative signs in the zodiac. One of your favourite hobbies is amateur dramatics, because most Leos adore being in the limelight. You may even have thought about becoming a professional actor because you enjoy treading the boards so much. You might also enjoy dancing, whether you go to regular classes or you simply love tripping the light fantastic with your partner. Travel appeals to you, especially if you can visit luxurious hotels in hot parts of the world. However, you're not very keen on roughing it! Clothes are very important to you, so you enjoy shopping for the latest fashions and you may also be an accomplished dressmaker.

 Virgo

One of your favourite pastimes is to keep up to date with your health. You're fascinated by medical matters and you enjoy reading books telling you how to keep fit. You may even try out all the latest eating regimes, hoping that you'll find one that suits you perfectly. This interest in health means you're keen to eat well, and you could enjoy growing your own vegetables. Even cultivating a few herbs in a windowbox will give you a sense of achievement and you'll be pleased to think they are doing you good. You have tremendous patience so you might enjoy fiddly hobbies that require great dexterity, such as knitting, needlepoint and sewing. You might also enjoy painting designs on china and glass.

Libra

Libra is a very sensual sign, so any hobbies that appeal to your senses are bound to go down well. You love delicious smells so you might enjoy learning about aromatherapy, so you can cure yourself of minor ailments and also create your own bath oils. You could also get a big thrill out of making your own cosmetics or soaps, and you might become so good at them that you give them away as gifts. You take great pride in looking good, so you enjoy visiting your favourite shops and keeping up with the latest fashions. Music is one of your great loves and you might play an instrument or sing. If not, you certainly appreciate other people's musical talents and you enjoy going to concerts and recitals.

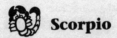 ## Scorpio

Whatever hobbies you choose, they have to mean a lot to you. You simply aren't interested in activities that don't carry an emotional meaning for you and you'd rather not bother with them at all. One pastime that's dear to the hearts of most Scorpios is wine-tasting. You might enjoy teaching yourself all about wine, either with the help of some good books or simply by drinking whatever appeals to you. You're fascinated by mysteries, and you could enjoy reading lots of whodunits or books on true crimes. You are also intrigued by things that go bump in the night, and you can't resist going on ghost hunts or visiting famous places that are known to be haunted.

 **Sagittarius**

You're one of the great collectors of the zodiac, whether you know it or not. You may not think that you collect anything at all, but other people will take one look at all your books and beg to disagree with you. Reading is one of your great pleasures in life and you're always buying books on your latest enthusiasms. Travel is something else that appeals to you, and you love planning where you're going to go next on holiday. You like to keep active and you enjoy outdoor sports in particular. Horse-riding is a classic Sagittarian activity, and you enjoy going to the races and having a little flutter. You also like activities that present you with a challenge – you're always determined to beat it!

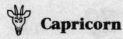 **Capricorn**

If you're a typical Capricorn you often take life rather seriously, so it's important for you to have lots of spare-time activities that allow you to relax. However, you've got to find the time first, and that means stopping work rather than burning the candle at both ends. Something that might appeal to you is rock-climbing, and you'll enjoy planning the strategy of how you're going to get to the top. Even a gentle walk amid mountain scenery does you a lot of good and helps you to relax. You're a very practical sign and you enjoy gardening. Not only does it help to ground you, you also like growing your own fruit and vegetables and then comparing the prices with those in the shops. Music helps you to unwind, and you'll love going to the opera or a glittering concert.

Aquarius

Most Aquarians have such a wide range of interests that almost anything is bound to appeal to you. You may go through phases, immersing yourself in one hobby for years until another one takes your fancy. However, you are only interested in activities that keep you intellectually stimulated and that teach you more about the world. You may go to lots of different evening classes, and you might even study for a degree in your spare time. Eastern philosophy could appeal, and you might also be an active campaigner for human rights. Astrology is a big hit with many Aquarians, and you'll enjoy teaching yourself all about it. Group activities are another interest, and you're an avid member of all sorts of organizations and societies.

THE YEAR 2000

 Friends and Lovers

It's going to be a wonderfully lively year, with lots to look forward to. Your feelings will run very deep during the first six weeks of 2000 and you will gain tremendous emotional satisfaction from being with people you care about. In fact, all of your priorities in life will have extra meaning for you until the middle of February, and they will give you more pleasure and contentment than usual.

Your social life will keep you very busy between February and June. You could receive more invitations than usual because you will be in great demand. There will be times when you long for an early night because you're not sure if you can keep up this demanding social pace for much longer! It will be delightfully easy to get on well with close relatives, neighbours and people that you see in the course of your daily routine. You might even be able to forge a fresh understanding with someone if you've fallen out with them recently or there has been a period of coolness between you. You might also hear some very good news from someone who lives far away or that you haven't seen in a while.

Pay close attention to your family and domestic life between August and September, because someone may be going through a bad time or you may simply derive great comfort from being surrounded by familiar faces and places. The rest of the year will be much more enjoyable and relaxed on the home front, and it's the perfect excuse to arrange a big family reunion or to welcome a new member into the family circle.

As a Piscean you are a born romantic, and you're certainly feeling that way in 2000. Although it's a fabulous year for drifting off on a wonderful, fluffy cloud of happiness, try to maintain some sense of reality. Otherwise there is a chance that you might misread the signals that someone is sending you, fall in love with love or indulge in fantasies that have no basis in fact. So keep your feet on the ground sometimes and all will be well!

Health

How are you feeling as you start the year? If you're feeling tired or below par, you should take extra care of yourself in January. Maybe you know that you ought to see a doctor or other health professional to discover what's wrong, or perhaps you would prefer to embark on a regime of your own devising. You certainly should not ignore any strange symptoms or ailments that have hung around for too long, because they will only prey on your mind until you get them sorted out. January is also an excellent time to give up a habit that isn't doing your health any good, such as smoking or drinking too much. You have increased willpower at this time so you stand a good chance of sticking to your resolve.

It's a year in which you need to keep busy, otherwise you will soon start to feel bored, fed up and possibly even depressed. If you do succumb to the blues, make sure you have a change of scene. Even a day trip or a weekend break could do the trick and make you feel better. If you would like to take more exercise, simple activities such as walking or cycling will do you a lot of good. Maybe you could leave the car at home sometimes and walk to the shops, or get off the bus one stop early to ensure that you take a little exercise every day.

There could be times in 2000 when worries and anxieties nag away at you. If this happens, try to confide in someone or put your thoughts down on paper. It won't do you any good to bottle up your feelings or brood on them.

 **Money**

Want to hear some good news? You start the year feeling very flush! You've got six weeks in which to make the most of financial opportunities so you can't afford to let the grass grow under your feet. It's a marvellous time to make a big investment in something, especially if you are spending money on things that will bring you pleasure or will grow in value over the years. You might also receive a lump sum or lots of small payments in the weeks leading up to the middle of February. However, it's also likely that you could spend a lot of money during this time, so take care if your finances are stretched at the start of 2000. You could be tempted to buy all sorts of nice things, whether you can afford them or not.

Spending money on improving your communications will be a wise investment between February and late June. How about buying a new phone, TV or computer? Perhaps you fancy linking up to the Internet or maybe you've got your eye on a new car? Buying anything that enables you to keep in touch with others will be money well spent during this time. You might also find that your phone bill is bigger than usual, because you'll enjoy having long chats on the phone.

Your home and family will be the main financial focus from the end of June onwards. This is the ideal time to invest your money in property, furniture or anything else connected with your home. For instance, you might decide to expand your living space in some way or you could carry out some home improvements. Be selective about what you throw away, because something that looks like junk to you could turn out to be valuable, especially if it's old. So think twice before chucking out that old vase that you've always hated. It could be worth something!

Career

If you want to get ahead this year you need to talk to other people. Communications are the key to your success in 2000, so don't keep your thoughts to yourself. This is especially important between January and August, when you will receive tremendous opportunities to make contact with influential people. Follow up these chances because they don't come along every day! Social events could also introduce you to some important contacts, so it's one of those years when you will never know who you are going to bump into.

It is also a marvellous year to put your thoughts down on paper and map out your ideas. Your job may involve a lot more writing than usual, or you could land a new job that involves communications of some sort. Negotiations and discussions will go well, as will meetings and interviews.

This is an important year to think about your goals and objectives. Are you happy with them? Are they still realistic? If you have lost interest in your ambitions, start revising them in 2000. A change of attitude on your part might lead to major changes in the direction of your life. This is especially likely if you were born between 1 and 7 March. If your birthday falls within these dates, you might see a change in your career this year or you could start to realize that your current occupation is no longer bringing you the satisfaction that it once did. You might also have to deal with a boss or authority figure who wants to have things all their own way or who is very difficult to deal with. But whenever your birthday falls, 2000 could be the year in which you gain increased confidence in your abilities or you finally reach a position of power. If so, it will be well deserved.

Your Day by Day Guide

JANUARY AT A GLANCE

Love	♥ ♥
Money	£ $
Career	💻 💻 💻
Health	☼ ☼

• *Saturday 1 January* •

The new millennium begins with you thinking very positively and constructively about your friendships and goals in life. It is an excellent day to meet up with people who share the same interests as you, so you can plan your forays together in the year ahead. This is also the ideal time to meet up with neighbours or siblings, especially if you feel the need to build bridges or cement relationships for the future.

• *Sunday 2 January* •

Even for a Pisces, you feel especially sensitive today and will not be interested in dealing with any day-to-day mundane matters. Now is the time to let your imagination soar and to indulge in some romantic revelry! Indeed, you will either be preoccupied with wooing the one you love or pondering upon the mysteries of life – a good opportunity to concentrate on whatever is really important to you.

• *Monday 3 January* •

Emotions run deep today and work is the area where you feel things most intensely. You'll want to reach out to others and show them how much you care about them. However, try not to worry if they don't return your strong feelings. You want to be recognized by the world today but beware of being so forceful that you put someone's back up.

• *Tuesday 4 January* •

You'll have the strength of your convictions over the next five weeks and will fight your corner as and when the need arises. You're not always renowned for your fighting qualities so you might surprise a few people – including yourself! An unexpected opportunity for career advancement may arise today, particularly through a female colleague or client. Be alert or you may miss the boat and regret the chance that came your way.

• *Wednesday 5 January* •

Your breadth of vision and ability to think up good schemes will not go unnoticed by those at work, so don't be afraid to put yourself forward. You also feel like having some fun, so why not meet up with an old friend? A night on the town could be just what you need. Also, you may want to fight someone else's battle, especially if you feel they've been treated badly.

• *Thursday 6 January* •

Today's New Moon highlights issues around friends and your goals in life over the next two weeks. You'll hear some news that reassures you about a friend and you'll want to sit down and discuss shared plans for the future. You're enthusiastic about a new scheme, and now is the ideal time to sort out the practical details. It's also a good time to make amends with a neighbour who has been difficult recently.

• *Friday 7 January* •

It looks as though self-indulgence will be the name of the game today, so why not give in to the inevitable? You'll want to be out having fun with friends, eating and drinking and, yes, you'll want to be spending your money as though there's an endless supply of it. On a more serious note, you'll want to show a friend how much you care about them, possibly by lending them some money.

• *Saturday 8 January* •

You may feel somewhat confused and distracted today, making it difficult to work out people's motives. Someone seems determined to make you feel guilty or miserable, and it might be worth pondering what they're really up to. Your sensitivity towards someone at work who is under considerable emotional stress will win you their lifelong friendship. With so many different activities today, try to set aside some time to reflect on what's going on.

• *Sunday 9 January* •

This is a day in which the focus is very much on your standing in the world and your response to it. Someone may be trying to manipulate you in a very subtle way, and you'll need to be strong to stand up to them. Or are you the one whose motives are questionable today? Have a close look at yourself and others right now, because it will be easy to fool yourself in some way.

• *Monday 10 January* •

Your intuition is running very strongly now and this is a good time to act on any hunches you may have about increasing your earning power. You will also find it easy to express your emotions in spontaneous and exuberant ways. It's not always easy for Pisceans to express themselves assertively, so it's especially important that you tell someone what you really think when you have such an ideal opportunity.

• *Tuesday 11 January* •

Watch out today because you're emotionally charged and this could get you into serious trouble with someone over money matters. This person wants to remain firmly in control and it's not a good idea to make them feel that you're trying to challenge their authority. On a positive note, friends and neighbours will feel full of affection for you, especially if you are offering them your help in some way.

• *Wednesday 12 January* •

Any problems in your work or concerning your reputation over recent days can be put right now when an unexpected opportunity lets you show the world what a star you really are. Others will notice your magnetic quality and appreciate your ability to bring an element of excitement into the current situation. This could have an amazing effect on your position at work. But don't spend all day slogging away – go out and party!

• *Thursday 13 January* •

Your well-known intuition goes into overdrive today as you pluck ideas out of thin air and show how resourceful you can be when you put your mind to it. You'll certainly be thinking creatively about ways to increase your income and you'll be surprised by the number of brainwaves you come up with. You might also come up with ways of improving efficiency at work that will win you the approval of your boss.

• *Friday 14 January* •

A woman you work with will show you how much she values you, but don't expect your friends to be quite so accommodating. It looks as though the communication wires have got crossed and you're none too pleased. An argument over money could be the problem so try to avoid lending or borrowing anything today, for the sake of your friendships. Apart from that, you should be brimming with confidence in your financial resourcefulness.

• *Saturday 15 January* •

No matter how hard you try to get on with your life, a combination of other people and unforeseen circumstances seems determined to stand in your way. Not only does everyone seem to be misunderstanding you and making you feel that you're losing your marbles, but some news that you hear today could leave you feeling very low. This is a day to take care of yourself and to make sure that you don't leave yourself open to misinterpretation.

• *Sunday 16 January* •

Communication is no problem today but can you afford the resulting phone bill? If not, this is a great day to meet up with friends for a lively time. You're full of ideas and schemes for the future, and you'll enjoy meeting up with other people who can help you to reach your goals, as they're sure to be carried away by your infectious enthusiasm. It's not a day to retire from the world!

• *Monday 17 January* •

You should be able to achieve any number of tasks today. You're ready to work hard and you can apply your mind in a much more focused way than usual. Other people will also be willing to cooperate with you now, because they can see precisely how determined you are. If you've been putting off writing a report or a letter, get out your pen now!

• *Tuesday 18 January* •

Don't be surprised if communications prove more complicated than usual over the next two weeks. Not that you'll care
about that today as you're feeling loving towards everyone,
especially at home and at work. You will love being at home,
and a sudden event will remind you how wonderful life can
be. It's a day to break the mould of expectations within your
family and to show them a side of yourself they seldom see.

• *Wednesday 19 January* •

To say that you're a powerhouse today would be an understatement! Your drive to assert yourself in the world and in
your work could lead to breathtaking results, as you'll leave no
stone unturned. The downside of this is that you may drive
yourself to the point of collapse and also meet the resistance of
someone who has the power to scupper your plans. This could
lead to a nasty battle of wills. Be careful.

• *Thursday 20 January* •

You may find yourself feeling more retiring and reserved at
times over the next few weeks, but not today. You want to
have fun at any price (literally!) and you have the drive and
enthusiasm to ensure that you get at least one other person to
join you. There's a twinkle in your eye and you're in the mood
for love. Head for the nearest party or gathering. Enjoy!

• *Friday 21 January* •

Today's Full Moon brings into focus a conflict between your
need to keep routines going and your urge to do more exciting
things. To avoid a sense of inner conflict, set aside some time
for your essential chores, before allowing yourself to drift off
into the world of your imagination. Listening to music, reading poetry or simply allowing your mind to wander is all you
want to do right now.

• *Saturday 22 January* •

Your sense of optimism (or is it blind faith?) and the joy and goodwill you exude right now ensures that today will prove very lucky for you. Whatever financial schemes are floating in your mind will be well received by people whose support you need, so don't be afraid to ask for a favour at the moment. Someone wants to help you, and it may be in more ways than one!

• *Sunday 23 January* •

You feel positive about your work today, even though it's traditionally the day of rest. You may even want to meet up with a colleague to show them how much you appreciate their company. You'll also want to spend some time considering how you can improve your general efficiency or your working environment. There may be a chance to show a neighbour how considerate you are.

• *Monday 24 January* •

Over the next few weeks, new friendships may begin and old ones will bring increased happiness. Today, though, you only want to retire into your own little dreams, as the world seems too busy for your liking. This would be an ideal opportunity to take time off from work and spend the day in some beautiful surroundings, allowing yourself to drift and dream.

• *Tuesday 25 January* •

For some unknown reason you could feel quite low today. You don't really want to talk to anyone and, if you do, the chances are that you'll feel misunderstood. Even worse, it seems that one of your neighbours or close relatives is out to criticize you and you're not really in the mood to challenge their opinions. Besides, they're not interested in your side of the story.

• *Wednesday 26 January* •

Someone will be quite suggestible to the ideas you put across today. Your intuition is working at full throttle and you know how other people are thinking. Any ideas you have for improving your position at work will go down well because your sense of purpose will be plain to all. Also, you'll see opportunities that others fail to notice, so this is a good time to make your move.

• *Thursday 27 January* •

Financial matters will occupy much of your attention today as someone wants you to become their partner in a joint venture. There's no doubting their sense of optimism about how things will work out, but you need to be quite sure that you won't be the one who ends up having to foot the bill if anything goes wrong. Although you will share this person's enthusiasm, think twice before committing yourself.

• *Friday 28 January* •

Today is an excellent chance to withdraw from your everyday world and draw up a new strategy for your life. You'll be amazed by the brilliant ideas popping out of your mind right now, so when better to stand back from things and allow a whole new perspective to present itself to you? Avoid sharing these ideas with anyone yet, as they're not ready to hear them.

• *Saturday 29 January* •

Try to avoid older friends and relatives today as they are bound to misunderstand you, and this will lead to outbursts that you can do without. It's a day to explore new situations – it doesn't matter what these are, provided they are new and untried. You've got oodles of energy right now, and you need to get out into the world and share your sense of excitement with others. Fancy booking a foreign holiday?

• *Sunday 30 January* •

Someone you work for is under a lot of pressure at the moment, and who better to reassure them of their worth than you. Sensitivity and gentle handling is what they need, and you prove to be exactly what the doctor ordered. Your heightened sensitivity is recognized by just about everyone you meet today, and it also makes you receptive to subtle ways of improving your situation in the world.

• *Monday 31 January* •

You're not yourself today, so there's no point in trying to pretend that you are. Every time you try to get through to someone it's like hitting your head against a brick wall, so why bother? Not only that, but it'll undermine your confidence in yourself and who needs that! Far better to spend the day alone and get on with jobs that have to be done. Leave the rest of the world alone!

FEBRUARY AT A GLANCE

Love	♥ ♥ ♥ ♥ ♥
Money	£ $ £
Career	💻 💻 💻
Health	☼ ☼ ☼ ☼ ☼

• *Tuesday 1 February* •

Your intuition is working flat out today and it's the perfect time to initiate fundamental changes at work. Anyone in authority over you will be responsive to your bright ideas, and these could lead to a bright future for all concerned. Similarly, if you've recently been having problems at work, this is a good day to raise your concerns. You're able to express yourself with power and sensitivity now.

• *Wednesday 2 February* •

You feel a sense of sober affection today towards friends, relatives and even your neighbours. This is an ideal time to tell a special friend just how much they mean to you – not in a gushy, romantic way, but based on the realization that your friendship is built on a rock-solid foundation. People will respond well to your advice today because they trust you and know that you're trying to help them.

• *Thursday 3 February* •

You're feeling particularly sensitive about a cherished plan today and will want to work towards making this dream come true. Fortunately, you're full of energy and optimism and have the drive to set the wheels in motion. You'll be forthright with others, so woe betide anyone who tries to tell you that you can't afford to indulge your emotions at the moment and enjoy yourself. You'll soon put them right!

• *Friday 4 February* •

Listen to your intuition and instincts today. Although your focus is very much on your inner world, you'll also receive some exciting hunches about how you can improve your financial situation. These ideas may come out of the blue but that's no reason to not take them seriously. In fact, you'll feel so positive about them that you'll wonder why you didn't think of them sooner.

• *Saturday 5 February* •

Over the next two months it will be much easier than usual to say what you mean, so now it's the perfect opportunity to leave others in no doubt about what is important to you. Today, though, is not a good time to start, as the New Moon is making you feel highly excitable but prone to being misunderstood by others. Spend time on your own, thinking creatively about how to improve things.

• *Sunday 6 February* •

You feel shocked and excited by the brilliance of your thinking today. Ideas come to you out of a clear blue sky, making you wonder at your inventiveness. Take note of these inspirations, even though the time is not yet ripe to act on them. That is because many of your ideas are so unusual for you that it would be wise to give yourself some time to process them all. You'll know when it's time to act.

• *Monday 7 February* •

Be careful how you approach those with power over you today, as you'll probably bite off more than you can chew if you try to outmanoeuvre them. Be as straightforward as you can, because this is definitely your best option. Use your common sense and make sure that you avoid any other approach because you'll soon be sussed out, and then all your good work will be undone.

• *Tuesday 8 February* •

You feel very close to a certain friend today, so why not arrange to meet up and show just how much they mean to you. Emotionally, you're ready to open up to those around you, and this is therefore a good time to talk about issues that you may not have felt able to mention recently. What's more, you now have the drive and determination to have the courage of your convictions.

• *Wednesday 9 February* •

Work and money-making schemes are likely to be your main focus today, and you're sure to come up with some wonderful ideas to improve both areas of your life. Ideas that apparently come out of nowhere will make you feel very positive about your future prospects, and you'll be able to share these with people whose opinions you respect.

• *Thursday 10 February* •

Everything you touch turns to gold today as you tap into a reservoir of wonderful hunches that give you the opportunity to increase your earning power in ways that you would never have imagined. Friends may try to discourage you, but don't take it personally. They have your best interests at heart but lack the vision or imagination to keep up with your money-making plans. Press on regardless!

• *Friday 11 February* •

Recent days have seen you brimming with plans to increase your income and finally the time is right to act. You feel positive and full of optimism, and this is the basis for all successful activity. You will always have to cope with pitfalls and people ready to discourage you, but nothing will stop you from believing that the moment is right for plucking. What's more, you won't forgive yourself if you miss the boat.

• *Saturday 12 February* •

Your energy is now thoroughly focused on realizing your financial dreams over the coming month. Today, you'll want to increase your networks and to make a solid foundation for your plans, because you realize how important it is to be thoroughly prepared. Other people, however, seem determined either to misunderstand you or to place obstacles in your way, leaving you feeling frustrated. All you can do is be as clear as possible.

• *Sunday 13 February* •

Watch out for complications today, especially if you are hoping to gain someone's support for your current ideas. Are you being as straightforward and honest with others as you'll like them to be with you, or is it the other way round? It certainly looks as though someone is trying to be coercive, or is not beyond using manipulation as a subtle method of getting their own way. Watch out!

• *Monday 14 February* •

Although this is Valentine's Day, you may feel that the pull between work and home prevents you from realizing what is really important to you. No matter what demands are placed on you at work, make sure you remember your loved one – or be prepared to face a stormy reception when you return home! People will be prone to misunderstanding you, so be careful. Plan something unusual and exciting for this evening, if you're staying in.

• *Tuesday 15 February* •

Over the next few months you'll seek ways to increase your knowledge of the world and to become more open when communicating with others. Today, you have warm feelings towards family members and you want to enjoy the sense of retreating from the world in order to be with them. It's a particularly nice day to be around children, provided you've got the energy to keep up with them!

• *Wednesday 16 February* •

If you've considered showing your beloved how much you really care recently, this is the time to do it. You can express your feelings easily without any fear that you'll be misunderstood, so why not go out for a romantic dinner and enjoy the time together. Children will give you great pleasure today and your advice to one of them may strike a chord, helping them through a tricky problem.

• *Thursday 17 February* •

Although your intentions may be honourable, today is not a good time to advise a close colleague on how to run their love life. Your head is in the clouds and you're likely to misread the situation. But don't let that stop you from enjoying your own romantic drama, as you feel full of infectious enthusiasm and definitely want to have some fun. It's also a good day to catch up with your backlog at work.

• *Friday 18 February* •

Although you feel like spending time on your own today, getting out and about will lift your spirits because everyone will want to cheer you up. It's also a day when you may have some brainwaves about how to improve your financial position. Although these ideas may seem strange, you'll be surprised to find how well they work out.

• *Saturday 19 February* •

Today's Full Moon puts close personal relationships on the agenda over the coming fortnight. It will be a great opportunity to show someone just how much you care about them. They're sure to respond to your personal magnetism, so don't hold back. In fact, the more extravagant the gesture, the more they'll love you for it. If you've ever considered writing a poem as a declaration of love, then grab pen and paper now.

• *Sunday 20 February* •

Life is sweet today, and you want to share that feeling with everyone you meet. You're interested in everything and everyone now and, what's more, you feel good about yourself too. People around you will pick up on this, so you can expect compliments all round as they respond to your positive energy. If you have important issues to discuss with someone, speak up now.

• Monday 21 February •

Have you ever felt that you were talking to a brick wall? That may be quite a familiar feeling over the next three weeks when communication wires get crossed, leaving everyone in a state of perpetual confusion. All you can do is try to be as straightforward and open as possible, but don't be surprised if people still misunderstand what you try to say.

• Tuesday 22 February •

You long to take a back seat from life and do something with mystical, spiritual or creative overtones today. You're enormously sensitive and need to find some way to express it, such as painting or dancing. You're also in love with love but will probably find these feelings are too intense to share with your beloved. You may prefer to show your love in less personal ways, such as through an act of charity.

• Wednesday 23 February •

The winds of change blow a sudden and unexpected opportunity your way today, especially if it allows you to work productively towards a new and beneficial position. The decisions you make with a partner look like bailing you out of a situation that was stuck in a rut. Now is the time to act on your instincts because there is no doubt you'll size up the situation with eerie accuracy.

• *Thursday 24 February* •

Your ability to see the great scheme of things and to feel philosophical about your life is enhanced today. It's just as well really, because you feel confused about everything else right now. You would rather be left alone but others make demands that you have to meet. This could leave you feeling quite depleted, particularly as a certain person seems determined to monopolize you with question after question.

• *Friday 25 February* •

No matter how hard you try to express yourself and share your feelings today, you'll end up wondering why you bothered. A neighbour, or someone you see on a daily basis, seems hell-bent on trying to drag you down into the same rut that they're in. After trying to placate them, the chances are that you'll give them a piece of your mind, which they probably deserve.

• *Saturday 26 February* •

The world is a beautiful place today. You exude a charisma that charms others and enables you to achieve your objectives with a minimum amount of effort. You're also sensitive to others and this quality will not go unnoticed. You may put yourself out or make a sacrifice in order to do someone a good turn.

• *Sunday 27 February* •

Charm and determination are an irresistible force, as you demonstrate so well today. You're determined to put plans for your financial prospects into action now and you know exactly how to do it. What's more, if you need someone's help, they'll be more than willing to lend a helping hand. This is because you approach them in a way that seduces rather than overpowers them.

• *Monday 28 February* •

There are times when we feel lonely, even when surrounded by people to whom we normally feel close. Unfortunately, this is one of those days. No matter how hard you try to reach out to others, you feel sad and misunderstood. Try not to take it all to heart, and realize that it's just a passing phase. Spend some time on your own, as this will help you to focus your thoughts.

• *Tuesday 29 February* •

Whatever you do today, ensure that you're scrupulously honest in your dealings with others. Any attempt to disclose or manipulate information will backfire on you and lose you the respect of someone whose support you rely upon. At the same time, you'll suss out anyone who may not be telling the whole story, because you'll be able to see what is really going on. Express yourself clearly now and you can achieve great things.

MARCH AT A GLANCE

Love	♥ ♥ ♥ ♥ ♥
Money	£ $ £ $ £
Career	💻 💻 💻 💻 💻
Health	☼ ☼ ☼ ☼ ☼

• *Wednesday 1 March* •

This is the ideal time to stand up and tell others exactly who you are and what you think. You're full of self-confidence and are ready to take centre stage. Don't waste this opportunity to give yourself a real confidence boost, and to raise your standing in the eyes of the world. People will be pleasantly surprised, as this is not your usual style.

• *Thursday 2 March* •

Your communication skills serve you well today as you can discuss serious issues in a way that inspires the confidence of others. A neighbour or close relative may turn to you for advice and you'll be only too happy to help out. If you need to negotiate or discuss anything of importance, try to do it now, as you'll probably achieve the desired outcome much more easily than you imagined.

• *Friday 3 March* •

Watch out for trouble at work because someone feels that you've got too big for your boots. Or maybe it's simply that they're on a big power kick and have decided to flex their muscles on you. Although it won't do a great deal for your self-esteem, you'd be wise to withdraw from any confrontation. In this situation, discretion is the better part of valour.

• *Saturday 4 March* •

A fantastic chance to increase your income may arise out of the blue today. It may be thanks to a creative idea that you have or it may be due to someone else presenting you with an opportunity because of the affection they feel towards you. In fact, you could also be given a romantic opportunity today, and even if you don't respond to it your morale will get a massive boost as you bask in the admiration of others.

• *Sunday 5 March* •

Get out and about and enjoy yourself today, because you're full of interest in everything and everyone. You're able to communicate easily with others right now, as you're sensitive to their feelings and able to express your sense of joy in a very down-to-earth way. Good news is likely to come along but, in spite of this, keep out of the way of someone who seems determined to have a go at you.

● *Monday 6 March* ●

Today's New Moon will fill you with confidence about your place in the world over the next two weeks. If you are a typical Piscean you are often thought of as a retiring person but this certainly won't be true in the days ahead as you prove that you can be as much of an extrovert as anyone else. Also, people will have to get up early to take advantage of you, as you will make very obvious.

● *Tuesday 7 March* ●

There are times when we're compelled to act for no apparent reason, and this is one of them. Some brilliant idea arising from who knows where will compel you to act in a way that you could have scarcely imagined. What's more, it may help you to increase your earning power. You will enjoy showing others, and yourself, just how positive you can be when you put your mind to it.

● *Wednesday 8 March* ●

The brilliance and forcefulness of your ideas cannot possibly go unnoticed by others as they realize how much you have to offer them. You'll probably be surprised by their quirky or unconventional nature. However, once you come to terms with this, you'll lose no opportunity in getting your ideas across to someone whose support you need in order to put them into action. Tread boldly and bring your dreams one step closer to reality.

● *Thursday 9 March* ●

This is another day in which to get out and share your ideas with others. You're positively brimming with brilliance and goodwill, so why hide your light under the proverbial bushel? Your mind is alert and open to new ideas, so this is the perfect time to explore any subject that has proved too difficult up to now. You will hear some news that inspires you with confidence and makes you want to shout it from the rooftops.

• *Friday 10 March* •

After the excitement of recent days, you'll want to shut up shop and be on your own today. Fat chance of this happening, however, as others force you to face up to your responsibilities. Something you hear will make you wish that you had a pair of earplugs handy. Try to avoid getting caught up in other people's problems today as it will be like trying to walk through treacle.

• *Saturday 11 March* •

You're particularly sensitive today, and something that's said in all innocence is likely to leave you feeling deeply hurt. You can't express yourself easily at the moment and this will prevent you talking to the person concerned in order to clarify the matter. Family members aren't much help either and you're likely to feel angry with a certain person due to their apparent insensitivity. Maybe it's simply that you're too touchy at the moment?

• *Sunday 12 March* •

Make the most of today's brilliant ideas. You'll need all the resourcefulness you can muster to resolve matters arising at home or at work. Someone seems determined to make you suffer and will try any trick in the book to manipulate you into being subservient to them. Fortunately, your canny insight enables you to see through them and avoid their underhand tactics.

• *Monday 13 March* •

The next few weeks will see your popularity soar as others recognize what a warm and affectionate person you really are. They will simply be responding to the energy that you exude. Right now, you're full of ideas and drive, especially around the house, but you'll also want to get out and enjoy yourself. A trip to the cinema or the theatre will do very nicely.

• *Tuesday 14 March* •

If you have children or feel close to some, spend some time with them today. They'll bring you great joy as they put you in touch with your own childlike nature, and you'll be able to teach them a great deal about some aspects of life. If you've been putting off writing a letter, put pen to paper now. You'll be amazed at how easy it is to set down your thoughts.

• *Wednesday 15 March* •

There are days when all you want to do is sit around and chat with people you like, and this is one of them. In fact, it'll be hard to do anything else because you're feeling affectionate and playful, and want to treat everyone with a light touch. Even if you gossip all day, as you might, no harm will come of it. If you need to sell yourself to the world, then this is your day.

• *Thursday 16 March* •

You are in a very idealistic and impractical mood today. You're full of noble intentions to help others, and will want to spend some time contemplating the deeper meaning of life. This is all well and good, but be aware of a slight tendency to be unreliable about yourself and others. Your head may be in the clouds but try to keep your feet firmly on the ground.

• *Friday 17 March* •

Watch out for erratic emotional reactions today, especially at work, as they may land you in hot water with colleagues who won't take too kindly to your stroppy attitude. It would be a shame to waste today's opportunities because you're full of enterprising ideas and are blessed with the energy to see them through. Be tolerant of those who don't understand your brainwaves – they'll support you soon enough.

• *Saturday 18 March* •

It's a day to sweep someone off their feet, unless you want to wait for them to do it to you! You're full of loving affection and are confident that other people share your feelings. As the old saying goes – smile and the world smiles with you! This is an excellent day to make friends with your neighbours and to catch up with close friends and relatives. You will also hear some news that fills you with joy.

• *Sunday 19 March* •

A long, serious discussion with a partner looks on the cards. Although you are feeling things deeply, this is tempered by a need to take a practical look at how things stand between you. This is a time when criticisms can be made without causing offence, as you're both feeling level-headed enough to avoid overreacting. You will be able to make some solid plans for your future together.

• *Monday 20 March* •

Today's Full Moon indicates your desire to balance your own needs with those of your partner. If you're a solo Pisces at the moment, you may feel quite lonely and imagine that everything would be better if you only had a partner. As always, the grass is greener on the other side of the fence! Whatever your emotional situation, you could be overwhelmed by a wonderful sense of beauty and spirituality over the coming fortnight.

• *Tuesday 21 March* •

You get an opportunity to make your mark today when others are amazed at your perceptiveness, particularly when it comes to financial affairs. This is also the perfect time to talk to someone about matters that have been too sensitive to mention recently. You're able to see things as they really are, yet you are in a forgiving mood and will be willing to do whatever it takes to improve relations.

• *Wednesday 22 March* •

Someone gets on your nerves today and you can expect to see red. It's highly likely that money is the cause of all the problems but try not to let things get out of hand between you. You may realize that you're not as sure of your ground as you first thought, so try not to burn your bridges. Words spoken in haste are not easily taken back.

• *Thursday 23 March* •

It will be much easier than usual to say what you think over the next six weeks, but remember that being assertive doesn't have to mean being aggressive. Be careful today as you're prone to acting in a slightly underhand manner in order to achieve your aims, and it's not likely to work out for you. Alternatively, someone in authority over you seems willing to use their power for their own ends. Tread warily!

• *Friday 24 March* •

This is a day to take stock of recent events, especially yesterday's, and to decide how to deal with any damage that may have been done. If you've been the guilty party, try to make amends for your actions. If you are the aggrieved party, try to be generous in spirit if the other person tries to say sorry. If they don't offer an olive branch you'll have the true measure of their real character.

• *Saturday 25 March* •

Your sense of optimism and goodwill is exactly what you need right now, and it enables you to reach out to others with warmth and affection. Try to get out and about and meet new people in your area, as you're full of curiosity and are open to new experiences. News that you hear today will prove reassuring, especially if it concerns a close relative, as it will show how much you mean to them.

• *Sunday 26 March* •

Thoughts of a spiritual nature could preoccupy you today. It's one of those times when you feel lifted out of your normal view of life and are able to see the world in a very different light. You may want to make some kind of sacrifice to help someone else out, but it won't feel like a sacrifice. Instead, you will feel joy in being able to give yourself to another person.

• *Monday 27 March* •

Your attention returns to the mundane world today and you'll be avidly seeking your fortune. Your direct approach should enable you to see your way through any obstacles that crop up, and will also help you to find ways to increase your income. Alternatively, you may decide to go on a spending spree, in which case you'll let nothing stand in your way – you're sure you'll be able to replenish the coffers.

• *Tuesday 28 March* •

Turbulence is on the horizon because a certain friend seems determined to rub you up the wrong way. Is it over money or are they simply trying to undermine your sense of self-worth? Whatever the problem, you'll brook no interference and will let them know this in no uncertain terms. Fortunately, other friends will rally round and show how much they value you.

• *Wednesday 29 March* •

A peaceful day beckons, so take advantage of the calm atmosphere. It's a good chance to spend some time with a close friend as they'll be sure to enjoy your company and will want to make you feel at home. Also, try to contemplate what has been going on in your life recently, and what changes you may need to make. Your ideals are important, so try to consider how you might achieve them.

• *Thursday 30 March* •

You need to keep your wits about you today as someone seems determined to outmanoeuvre you. Are they deliberately trying to wrong-foot you, or do they feel that you've got too big for your boots and need cutting down to size? Be careful about what you say because you don't want to speak out of turn or make the situation worse. Be as straightforward as possible.

• *Friday 31 March* •

It's another day in which you need to be careful about how you communicate with others. The problem is that you feel so confused that you may end up saying things you didn't mean. This is a time for writing poetry rather than memos, due to your creative but dreamlike state. Don't allow yourself to be caught up in idle gossip as you could easily get the wrong end of the stick.

APRIL AT A GLANCE

Love	♥ ♥ ♥
Money	£ $ £ $ £
Career	💻 💻 💻
Health	☼ ☼ ☼ ☼

• *Saturday 1 April* •

News that you hear, or events in your neighbourhood, will affect you in a very emotional way today. If any response is required, you're ready for action and willing to offer any help that might be needed. Your mind is alert and you're interested in everything going on around you. It's a good day to tackle any mental activities for which you haven't recently had the time or energy.

• *Sunday 2 April* •

Seldom has there been a better opportunity to make your mark in the world and increase your income at the same time! You're full of drive and determination to achieve whatever task you set for yourself. Because you believe in yourself, people whose support you need will be bowled over by your self-confidence and the air of power and authority you exude. Your mind is fully focused, so reach out for your goal.

• *Monday 3 April* •

Savour and enjoy today because you feel good in yourself and warm towards everyone you meet. Other people will tune into your friendly and non-threatening disposition, and will be sure to reflect back to you the affection that you give out. Someone in need may turn to you for help because they know that you're the best person to approach, and they are absolutely right!

• *Tuesday 4 April* •

Thoughts of how to improve your earning power will occupy your attention today. You feel inspired by ideas that make you realize you may have more control over your destiny than you previously thought. What's more, you're feeling bold enough to discuss your ideas with people who can help you to achieve them. They're sure to support you, so act on the power of your convictions.

• *Wednesday 5 April* •

Money matters are on your mind and your current inventiveness will make you realize how rich the pickings can be if you're willing to act on your hunches. It's as though you're able to tap into a reservoir of new ideas that you'd never previously been aware of. If you go shopping today, don't be surprised if you feel driven to buy some outrageous items that you'd never have previously considered.

• *Thursday 6 April* •

You come into your own today because your positive and powerful thinking reverberates throughout your environment. You're interested in everyone you meet, particularly if they'll listen to your views on the problems of the world. Not that you're willing to play the role of armchair philosopher – that's far too passive. This is a day running on adrenalin. Be careful if you're driving, as your impetuous urges could get the better of you.

• *Friday 7 April* •

You'll certainly be connecting with the world today but there may be a few loose wires! You're highly excitable and this adds a frantic and frenetic tension to the way in which you communicate with others – you may leave them feeling shell-shocked. Stop your mind from racing away, even though you'll be excited by the content of your thoughts.

• *Saturday 8 April* •

You're aware of how the different stresses and strains of work and home can leave you feeling that you're on the rack and being pulled in two directions at the same time. Try to put these worries to one side and relax. How about a shopping spree, especially if it involves buying beautiful items for your home? Alternatively, go somewhere serene and beautiful and enjoy the tranquillity. What about a day at the seaside?

• *Sunday 9 April* •

Expect the unexpected today, especially when it comes to how you think about yourself. A sudden revelation makes you realize that you may not be quite the person you thought you were. Don't worry though, as it'll feel as though your ball and chain has been unlocked and you're free to be the person that you want to be. Too often we trap ourselves in our fears and low self-expectations, but you aren't doing that today.

• *Monday 10 April* •

It looks as though the urge to go on a spending spree will prove irresistible, as you want to improve your appearance and show a certain person just how attractive you can be. Get out into your local neighbourhood today and you'll be amazed at how much fun you'll have. People you may not normally talk to will prove stimulating and remind you how magical the world is when you have a positive outlook.

• *Tuesday 11 April* •

There is friction in the air as a loved one gives you grief for not spending enough time, and perhaps money, on them. Don't worry, however, as you will melt their mood like sunshine on chocolate. As if by magic, you'll mesmerize them with your loving affection and attentiveness without even trying. If you're single, now is the time to throw doubt aside and express your feelings to someone you admire.

• Wednesday 12 April •

Time spent with children today will make you feel young at heart. Although there is a chance that you could feel under the weather and out of sorts, it won't stop you enjoying your work. You feel creative, especially if you are thinking of ways to earn some extra money. A colleague will turn to you for support as they recognize how warm-hearted you are, and you'll enjoy giving them some wise advice.

• Thursday 13 April •

You can make great progress in your work today and win the respect of both colleagues and those in authority. You're open and direct, and able to express yourself in a powerful manner, but only if you use charm rather than force. You may feel frustrated by someone's reluctance to accept your point of view, but it would be best to leave them to their own devices as otherwise you'll only blow up in frustration.

• Friday 14 April •

After the almost manic way you felt yesterday, you now have the opportunity to relax and consider your position. Your thinking over the next few weeks will be largely focused on working out ways to increase your income. No opportunity will pass you by as your curiosity will enable you to explore all sorts of options that you wouldn't normally have the time or interest to consider.

• *Saturday 15 April* •

Communication with others takes on a very serious note today as you struggle to find exactly the right thing to say. Although you're full of good ideas about how to improve things, especially at work, you may feel a deep sense of self-doubt concerning your intelligence and your ability to make yourself understood. Try not to lash out in anger if someone riles you – that's exactly what they're hoping for.

• *Sunday 16 April* •

Whatever you do today, don't commit yourself to any financial venture as you're likely to misunderstand what you're letting yourself in for. The information you receive is likely to be fundamentally inaccurate, and this could leave you seriously out of pocket. Apart from this, you're feeling too emotional to make sound, rational decisions and someone may want to take advantage of this. Try to avoid idle gossip – it will only drain you.

• *Monday 17 April* •

You will be full of self-belief today if you listen to your intuition, so make sure you keep yourself tuned in. As well as being drawn towards anything artistic or spiritual, and wanting to help others, you're full of fantastic ideas for improving your income. This may be through speculation or increasing the effectiveness of how you work. One thing is for sure – your actions won't go unnoticed.

• *Tuesday 18 April* •

Someone may try to wrap you round their little finger today. Are they after your money or your heart? No matter, for you're more than a match for them, as you see straight through them and know exactly what they're up to. Don't sign any document that will commit you until you've had the time to look very closely at the small print. This will annoy someone who wants to put one over on you, so be warned.

• *Wednesday 19 April* •

The next few weeks are the perfect time to enjoy being with other people. You're full of bright ideas, optimism and sensitivity towards others, but you're in danger of spreading yourself too thin. While you want to help a certain person, don't make any promises that you can't keep. Other people intend to occupy you with trivial chatter, and you may end up achieving nothing but a guilty conscience.

• *Thursday 20 April* •

Today's events are a double-edged sword, as you're full of brilliant ideas and able to apply them forcefully and productively. However, you're also prone to acting impulsively and wilfully, and this could be your undoing because you're not prepared to wait for the right moment before taking action. If you can curb your impatience, you can expect to achieve great things. Take particular care if you're driving, because you could be tempted to take risks.

• *Friday 21 April* •

There are times when we can affect other people in subtle ways that are hard to imagine. Today is one of them, and people that you want to impress will be bowled over by your presence. Enjoy yourself as people sing your praises but don't get too carried away by it. The chances are that you won't, as you're too concerned for the well-being of someone less fortunate.

• *Saturday 22 April* •

This is another day in which you reach out to the world and are received with open arms. Great! You exude a powerful magnetic presence that mesmerizes everyone, and leaves them like putty in your hands. Fortunately, you're honest in the way you deal with people today, and reach out to them with warmth and affection. This, in turn, ensures that your goodwill is returned and an exciting day is ensured. Enjoy!

• *Sunday 23 April* •

Whatever you touch seems to turn to gold at the moment, though you haven't got a clue why this should be. Life is full of exciting possibilities this April, and your self-esteem is soaring as you realize how much other people admire you. Not only that, but a sudden and unexpected opportunity to reawaken your love life may come along. What's more, you're ready to take the plunge!

• *Monday 24 April* •

If you've lost contact with a good friend, why not write to them or pick up the phone? You are in a very chatty and communicative mood, so it's a great opportunity to catch up on all the gossip. You might hear something that makes you feel on top of the world. Don't keep it to yourself because everyone will be happy to share in your good fortune.

• *Tuesday 25 April* •

Trust your intuition today because you'll be amazed at the results! It's as though you can tap into a vast reservoir of fantastically original ideas that have never occurred to you before. Now is the time to think about ways of increasing your income. You can be sure that you'll have no shortage of possibilities. Although some of these may be unusual, they may still provide the answer to your problems.

• *Wednesday 26 April* •

This is a day when you're best advised to retire from the world and spend the time in contemplation, or to get involved in some form of artistic work where you can be alone. Being with other people at the moment will only stir up feelings of confusion and inadequacy, as you'll feel that everything you say or do is being misunderstood. This will only make you feel ever more vulnerable, so try to avoid it.

• *Thursday 27 April* •

Your sensitivity towards the needs of others and your ability to see the main chance combine well today. This gives you the ability to impress someone whose influence is very important, as they'll be uplifted by your ability to tune into the way they're feeling. In spite of this, you'll feel up and down emotionally because of something that you hear or read, and this may leave you feeling frayed around the edges.

• *Friday 28 April* •

You might just as well accept the fact that nothing will stop you going on a shopping spree today. Your mind is preoccupied with how you can improve your appearance, and what better way than to update your wardrobe! You are also interested in the way you get on with other people now. You want them to like and respect you, and the best way for that to happen is for you to be your true self.

• *Saturday 29 April* •

Make sure you don't overstep the mark with someone who has the power to bring you crashing down to earth. You can be sure they won't be taking prisoners as far as you're concerned. Apart from this tricky matter, it looks like being a good day. You feel open to others and will want to get out and about,

meeting as many people as possible. Close family and neighbours can all be guaranteed to cheer you up.

• Sunday 30 April •

Your mind will be particularly alert over the next two weeks,
and today finds you full of dynamic thoughts but also down to
earth in the way you use them. Someone, possibly a close
relative, looks to you for help about a problem they have, and
you'll be only too willing to step into the breech. If you've
fallen behind with any letters or phone calls, make up for lost
time now while you're so full of mental energy.

MAY AT A GLANCE

Love	♥ ♥ ♥
Money	£ $
Career	💻 💻
Health	☼ ☼

• Monday 1 May •

Over the next few weeks you will truly value your ability to
tune into other people and recognize when they're in need of
help. And sure enough, someone needs your help today.
Unknown to you, there's a spin-off because your good work
will come to the attention of someone who'll prove to be a
useful ally and may, in turn, help you in ways you would
never have imagined.

• Tuesday 2 May •

Expect your routines to be interrupted by unusual and exciting happenings today. Not that you'll mind, as it will make for
an interesting day. Also, you'll be buzzing with creative,

intuitive insights that will make you feel good about yourself. Your ideas will be red-hot and may even help you to find a new way of earning some extra cash, even though the prospect may seem unlikely at the moment.

• *Wednesday 3 May* •

Although you're full of wonderful ideas, you can be sure that others will accuse you of building castles in the sand now. They'll find you vague and confused, and are likely to misunderstand much of what you say or do. For this reason, it's essential that you think carefully before you speak or act in order to avoid any communication breakdowns.

• *Thursday 4 May* •

Any misunderstandings that happened yesterday will come home to roost today. You may again be accused of overreaching yourself, due to a misplaced belief that everything will turn out for the best. Make sure that you are forthright and down-to-earth to avoid getting any flak. This will ensure that no one can accuse you of trying to take advantage of the situation.

• *Friday 5 May* •

Domestic bliss is interrupted today when someone blows their top over something small and trivial. Fortunately, things calm down as quickly as they erupted. There is nothing like a good argument to clear the air, and that's certainly the case today. You may even find that, once the dust has settled, you feel much closer to the person with whom you temporarily fell out. It's an excellent day to plan new colour schemes if you're thinking of doing some redecorating.

• *Saturday 6 May* •

Watch out for a major communications glitch with someone to whom you feel very close. Is one of you trying to pull the wool over the other one's eyes, or is it simply that your wires have temporarily become crossed? Don't let your hypersensitivity get the better of you, otherwise you'll create all sorts of strange scenarios in your mind. Try not to let someone's sob story get you entangled in their problems.

• *Sunday 7 May* •

You're feeling almost childlike in your affections today as you reach out to others with a warm heart. Indeed, it's an excellent time to be around children, as you're able to relate well to them and they'll love you for it. You're also extremely creative at the moment, so try to find some way to express yourself. At the very least, you'll enjoy a visit to the theatre, cinema or some other artistic entertainment.

• *Monday 8 May* •

What matters to you today is how able you are to share your philosophy of life with others. It may be homespun, or a variety of opinions, but you'll want to discuss it avidly with everyone you come across. Your optimism and cheerfulness rubs off on them, and ensures that the day will be very special, as you find meaning and significance in everything that happens now.

• *Tuesday 9 May* •

Although you won't feel as buoyant and extrovert as yesterday, you'll still be preoccupied with trying to make sense of the world around you. Unfortunately, though, your light-heartedness has left you and everything will seem much heavier, as you're now aware of how difficult life can be at times. Don't expect others to reassure you. Far from it, in fact, as you may find everyone rather hard going.

• *Wednesday 10 May* •

Someone seems determined to misunderstand you today, and this makes you want to give them a piece of your mind because you have no time for their games. Try to restrain yourself, even though this means biting your lip. News that arrives later in the day will make you realize that you could have dropped an enormous clanger. Concentrate on your work instead, as your efforts will not go unnoticed, and will give you a sense of achievement.

• *Thursday 11 May* •

Nothing that anyone might say will stop you from telling a certain person what you think of them when they try to put the shackles on you. This is a day when you'll brook no interference as you're determined to do whatever you want, rather than kowtow to anyone. What's more, anyone who stands in your way will get a verbal battering that will be as sudden as it is unexpected.

• *Friday 12 May* •

Although someone seems to be placing obstacles in your way, leave them to their own devices now. Life is too short to bang your head against brick walls. Instead, enjoy your time with others who recognize your qualities, and who don't want to play mind games with you. They'll make you realize that life is all about enjoying ourselves and bringing pleasure to others, not making things more difficult than they already are.

• *Saturday 13 May* •

The best advice for today is to keep out of the way of everyone, with the exception of those at home. You can be sure that communications will prove frustrating, so try to keep yourself to yourself whenever possible. Take care when driving because you're not overloaded with patience at the moment. Time spent at home on your own or with those you want to be with will prove reassuring.

• *Sunday 14 May* •

This is a good day for tackling any outstanding financial matters because you'll get a lot of help from other people. If you're discussing joint financial matters, trust your own judgement as your intuition is spot on. Family members will prove particularly helpful, so don't be afraid to seek their advice or assistance. Your financial acumen will also ensure that others regard you with considerable respect. Don't be surprised if you lend money to someone in a mess.

• *Monday 15 May* •

Your intuition is working brilliantly, so you can be sure that no one will pull a fast one on you. Not only will you have some great ideas for making money, but your love life may also move up a notch. Thanks to your heightened awareness, you'll know exactly how to make someone feel good about themselves. Not only that, they'll then feel better about you too.

• *Tuesday 16 May* •

Don't let the world get you down today when you suffer from a sudden crisis of confidence. Your whole philosophy of life seems to be under threat, as you try to make sense of the emotional impressions passing through your mind at the moment. You may feel confused or unsure of yourself, so try not to take things too seriously because you could be worrying about nothing.

• *Wednesday 17 May* •

After yesterday's hiccup, you're now ready to restore a sense of sanity into your thinking. You are thinking very clearly yet, strangely enough, others may feel that you're somewhat dreamy. Trust your judgement, especially if you have to give someone advice. You're feeling so positive today that you can expect to attract others like bees to honey. What a great excuse to go out and enjoy yourself!

• *Thursday 18 May* •

Someone you thought you could trust shocks you to the core by their actions today, but you are even more unsettled by what they say. They have either gone back on their word or, at the very least, changed their mind about something important to you. This is likely to leave you deeply saddened, and today's Full Moon simply intensifies your emotions. Rest assured that things will improve before too long.

• *Friday 19 May* •

Conflicts at home or at work seem unavoidable today unless you make a real effort to clear the air with someone. The trouble is that this is easier said than done, as you can't discuss a problem if the other person denies there is anything wrong. Dig away at them until you get to the bottom of the matter. You've got great energy and drive at the moment, so no task will be beyond you now.

• *Saturday 20 May* •

Your energy levels are so high that you must keep on the go now, otherwise you'll explode. The best way to do this is to keep busy and do lots of physical or therapeutic tasks. At the very least, go for a long and fast walk if you start to feel angry or jittery. If involved in anything needing drive and energy, you're sure to succeed. However, don't take anything for granted, as things could go wrong when you least expect it.

• Sunday 21 May •

A day of calm is on the cards, and it's more than welcome in the light of recent events. You have either achieved a great deal or you are feeling shell-shocked by what has happened. If it's the latter, you'll have the opportunity over the next few days to repair a damaged relationship. Now is the time to ponder on what you want to do and decide whether or not that relationship is worth salvaging or whether it's time to say farewell.

• Monday 22 May •

Friends rally round you today and show how much they appreciate you. Not only will this make you feel cheerful and optimistic, it will also soothe your feelings after all the recent upsets. You're able to get your ideas across to others easily, so take this opportunity to clear up any recent mis-understandings. Also, get out and about, especially with good friends, because you'll have a great time.

• Tuesday 23 May •

Someone close to home hasn't been very friendly recently but they now want to regain your affection, and they'll bend over backwards to achieve it. It would seem churlish to make them suffer further when you also want to patch things up. Don't waste the opportunity, as otherwise things will only go from bad to worse. The problem is that you both want the other one to make the first move! Don't let this result in a stalemate.

• Wednesday 24 May •

It's not every day that you're willing to sacrifice yourself for others, but you'll do so today – and you'll hit the jackpot as a result. Someone with influence sees your behaviour and will want to show their appreciation. Your mind is working brilliantly, and others will be amazed at your suggestions for changing things at home.

• *Thursday 25 May* •

You want to jump out of your cage today and leave your world behind. While it may seem an attractive prospect, you can be sure that someone is going to make you realize that things aren't quite that simple. The lesson they'll teach you is that real freedom is found in overcoming problems rather than running away from them. Deep down, you know they're right.

• *Friday 26 May* •

Get set for a day of dramas worthy of a soap opera – unless you can keep your cool while everyone else goes crackers. Although you'd like to have some time to yourself, commitments at home and at work lie heavily on your shoulders. What's more, everyone concerned seems determined to get their pound of flesh from you, so don't expect any favours unless you agree to their terms.

• *Saturday 27 May* •

This is a great day to savour your ideals and realize that home is still where the heart is, in spite of any bickering. You feel loving compassion towards your family or those with whom you live, and you want to show them how deeply your feelings go. If possible, have a change of scene today, especially if you can visit somewhere lovely, because you will be inspired by the natural beauty of the world.

• *Sunday 28 May* •

This is a great day to deal with all outstanding communication matters that you've been putting off recently. You're able to combine a sense of optimism with prudence, giving you the confidence to achieve your tasks without being overawed by the amount of work involved. Although you'd rather lounge around and generally enjoy yourself, you'll only feel guilty afterwards. So you know what you've got to do!

• *Monday 29 May* •

Whatever spare time you have today will almost certainly be spent in your local shops. Anything you buy for yourself will win the admiring glances of others, and you'll also want to buy something to brighten up the house. Your choice of colours may surprise you, as you're in the mood to act boldly. You have the opportunity to impress someone at work, and can rest assured of a warm reception at home.

• *Tuesday 30 May* •

Your awareness of beauty is magnified today, and you'll be happy to spend the day dreaming of ways to improve your home. You're also incredibly sensitive to the feelings of others and will want to show them how much you care for them. If this involves making sacrifices, it won't seem like it. You feel particularly affectionate towards family members, and will enjoy the time you spend with them.

• *Wednesday 31 May* •

Having observed your good nature yesterday, someone in your environment seems determined to seize the main chance and take advantage of you. Be careful, as they may play all sorts of tricks in order to bewilder you. You're not really up to dealing with the world today as you feel hazy in your thoughts and would rather be left to wander around in your dreams. Don't make any irreversible decisions today.

JUNE AT A GLANCE

Love	♥ ♥ ♥ ♥
Money	£
Career	💻 💻
Health	☀ ☀ ☀ ☀

• Thursday 1 June •

You find yourself at the mercy of opposing forces today, when both your family and your job place seemingly impossible demands upon you. Try not to react to other people's attempts to coerce you against your will. At the same time, you need to make it quite clear that you're not prepared to be anyone's doormat. By remaining calm but aware, you should be able to stay in control of the situation.

• Friday 2 June •

Events at home or in the family circle keep you on your toes today. Someone seems determined to use all their charm to ensure that they can wrap you round their little finger. No chance of that though, as you're only too aware of their real motives. You're feeling dynamic and adventurous so, if you're working on your home, you might suggest some dramatic or drastic changes. Have you thought of knocking down a few walls?

• Saturday 3 June •

Yet again, someone at home seems to be playing tricks, but are you sure you're the innocent party? Certainly, someone is being quite selfish in their lack of consideration for others, and not beyond using their sexual charm to attain their ends. Now is the time to bring matters over the last three days to a head so that you can move forward without hidden agendas. This will lead to changes that you'll find amazing.

• *Sunday 4 June* •

If there are any children in your life, you'll thrive in their company now. If not, then enjoy your own childlike nature by indulging yourself in playful or creative activities that are a lot of fun. A trip to the cinema is the very least that you deserve. If you're in love, don't miss the opportunity to show it. You can express your feelings very clearly now.

• *Monday 5 June* •

This is another excellent day for communicating your thoughts and feelings. Not only will your optimism and sense of fun prove infectious, you're also able to exercise good judgement over any matters where careful consideration is needed. Although you'll want to enjoy yourself with other people, you also want to achieve some tangible results and prove to them just how shrewd you really are.

• *Tuesday 6 June* •

Although you may be troubled by worrying thoughts either concerning your health or work, don't worry. Others will be amazed at how productive and insightful you turn out to be, and will look to you for support. Peace and love abound on the domestic front as someone goes out of their way to show just how much they care about you. Savour the moment!

• *Wednesday 7 June* •

Batten down the hatches at work. Your schedule is likely to be thrown into sudden chaos, making you feel highly impulsive and irritable. Although someone has assured you that they can be relied on, this may prove a gross exaggeration and could leave you in the lurch. The one good thing is that you're full of energy, so don't waste time fretting about others. Get on and do the job yourself.

• *Thursday 8 June* •

It's a day in which you want to share your thoughts and feelings with others, especially close loved ones or children. It's also an excellent time to go shopping for clothes, especially if you find something that makes you look as young as you feel right now. Make sure that your spree doesn't eat into your work time, as someone will be only too happy to point their finger at you.

• *Friday 9 June* •

Don't expect tranquillity at home today and you won't be disappointed. Either you or a loved one seems hell-bent on stirring things up over anything and everything. Are you sure that you're not the one who's causing the tricky atmosphere? If not, then all you can do is be as reasonable as possible, and don't let their antics ruffle your feathers. That would only make them feel they were right after all.

• *Saturday 10 June* •

Your insight and intuition will stagger everyone today, including you, as you show an uncanny ability to work out what is really going on. Your sensitivity, plus your uncompromising honesty, enables you to spell out some home truths to someone who'll respect you for being so straightforward. Also, you'll go out of your way to give practical help to someone who's in need of your support.

• *Sunday 11 June* •

This is a day to savour the love of family and close loved ones, and also to build bridges if you've fallen out with someone recently. However unlikely it seems, almost any relationship can be redeemed today, provided you show goodwill and a generosity of spirit. You may also have to be prepared to make the first move. You're full of love, so share it while you can.

• *Monday 12 June* •

Don't hesitate to seek out the advice of a certain family member today before making any important financial decisions. You can be sure of a forthright response which, although perhaps not the feedback you wanted to hear, will prove to be worth its weight in gold. This is not a good time to trust your own judgement because it's likely to be distorted by confused notions and wishful thinking. It's a day for dreaming rather than doing.

• *Tuesday 13 June* •

You're full of bright ideas for the future now, and will want nothing more than to share them with others. Don't be surprised if yesterday's dreams result in you booking that exotic foreign holiday you've always promised yourself. However, be prepared for certain people to tick you off for being so extravagant, as they see it. Right now, you're in no mood to negotiate your dreams away with anyone.

• *Wednesday 14 June* •

There are times when, no matter how hard you try, others seem determined to misunderstand you. Is this because you've been too sloppy in your thinking and have overlooked certain vital issues? If so, you'll have to take other people's criticism as fair comment. Similarly, if others make certain commitments to you at the moment, don't be surprised if they all backfire. In general, watch out for communication problems.

• *Thursday 15 June* •

Your heightened intuition and the affection which other people feel for you all add up to a fabulous day for you. If you want to make your mark on the world or stake your claim for a pay rise, then now is the time to act. You can be sure that those in authority will respond towards you in a sympathetic manner. Similarly, if someone needs your help, you'll be happy to do what you can.

• *Friday 16 June* •

Today's Full Moon throws a spanner in the works as you desperately seek out ways to honour your commitments to both your family and colleagues. You might as well accept that this may prove an impossible task. Perhaps family matters will have to wait until tomorrow when the weekend starts. Don't expect to earn any gratitude at home, although your endeavours at work will not go unnoticed.

• *Saturday 17 June* •

To describe life at home as anything less than fraught would be an understatement, as someone seems hypersensitive and thinks you're to blame. Maybe there's some truth in their accusations, and you could have been less impulsive and more considerate? Although you feel impatient and annoyed by other people's actions, try to see things from their point of view, and prove that you're not as uncooperative as they believe.

• *Sunday 18 June* •

Avoid falling out with a good friend today as you may disagree with each other over some petty issue, such as how to spend your time together. You're prone to feeling touchy and irritable, and are likely to interpret any difference of opinion as a major issue. It won't be easy for you to express your feelings, so anything you say may well be misunderstood. Try not to take yourself too seriously!

• *Monday 19 June* •

Any misunderstandings with a friend yesterday are now easily resolved, as you feel full of goodwill. You're also able to see how you may have contributed to the problem. Thanks to good humour combined with a large dose of common sense, all outstanding grievances will dissolve like sugar in tea. In general, it's an excellent day for all types of communication. You're able to combine optimism with pragmatism, and resolve any difficulties that may arise.

• *Tuesday 20 June* •

If you can leave your responsibilities behind you and do something relaxing today, you'll have a wonderful time. In fact, you desperately need time on your own now, in order to wander down the corridor of your dreams. Not that you won't be able to cope with whatever life may throw at you. It's simply that we all need the opportunity to recharge our batteries, and this is a good day for you to do just that.

• *Wednesday 21 June* •

Try not to let today's communication hiccups get to you. Losing your temper with whoever is responsible won't improve the situation, but may well lose you their respect. Instead, make a point of getting out and having some fun. If no one close to home is available to provide such entertainment, try painting or dancing, or maybe just go out with some friends. You never know what might happen!

• *Thursday 22 June* •

An exciting day is on the cards. Wear your heart on your sleeve and meet the world with a sense of hopeful expectancy! Your sunny and affectionate mood will rub off on others, and ensure that they'll be happy to provide the fun and excitement that you crave. Don't hesitate to tell a certain person how much you love them, as the chances are that it will make their day, as well as yours.

• *Friday 23 June* •

Step away from centre stage today because someone seems keen to pull you back into line. Tread carefully at work, as a person with influence will not be pleased if you stand up for yourself. Discretion is the better part of valour at times like this. Instead, try to enjoy the company of someone with whom you can let your hair down!

• *Saturday 24 June* •

This is a great chance to speak your mind and generally get your ideas across. You're feeling full of infectious good humour, but also aware of the need to be sensible and practical in your dealings with others. In other words, it's the perfect recipe for any wheeling and dealing that you need to perform! Other people are sure to be captivated, not only by your buoyant mood but also by your common sense and mastery of detail.

• *Sunday 25 June* •

The yearning for pleasure at any price won't come cheap today when you throw caution to the wind. Although the best things in life are free, the most beautiful and fun things often cost an arm and a leg. What's more, those around you will want you to cough up the cash to make sure that they have as much pleasure as you. Prepare to face your bank manager tomorrow!

• *Monday 26 June* •

Although you may feel shocked and irritable when you think about yesterday's extravagances, your mind will soon be buzzing with brilliant ideas about how to make up for them. Not only will you be amazed at your ingenuity, you will also be staggered by the speed with which you put your new schemes into operation. As the old saying goes, necessity is the mother of invention!

• *Tuesday 27 June* •

Despite any apprehensions you have, today promises to be a lot of fun. You reach out to others with warmth in your heart, and receive it back by the bucketful! Being with lovers, children, doing your own creative work or simply going out and having fun with friends are great ways to enjoy yourself now. Whatever you do, you'll want to share your thoughts and feelings with others, as a sign of your affection for them.

• *Wednesday 28 June* •

Your impatience and erratic emotional mood may get the better of you today, making you sharp and cutting when dealing with other people. The problem is that you're not willing to go at the same pace as others, and this is likely to result in a lot of frayed tempers. Someone digs in their heels, and you'll end up realizing that your impetuosity has lost you more than you stood to gain. Tread warily!

• *Thursday 29 June* •

After yesterday's difficulties, your good humour returns with a healthy dose of dignified humility. This will help you to make any amends that are necessary. Nevertheless, you'll feel torn between the devil and the deep blue sea when it comes to balancing your work with your domestic responsibilities. Something has got to give, and that means someone won't be happy.

• *Friday 30 June* •

Unexpected and exciting events disrupt your domestic routines today. Don't worry, though, as they're sure to be positive and beneficial, and will make you realize how much fun life can be when you're willing to live from moment to moment. Your mind is very creative now, especially when it comes to finding ways of making your home life more exciting or satisfying.

JULY AT A GLANCE

Love	♥ ♥ ♥ ♥ ♥
Money	£ $
Career	💻 💻
Health	☼ ☼

• *Saturday 1 July* •

Today's New Moon promises plenty of fun and frivolity, so get all dolled up and get out and enjoy yourself. Do anything that will bring you pleasure, and then you'll be a source of sunshine for anyone you meet. As if all this is not enough for one day, you're full of energy and drive, so you might decide to set yourself some impossible goals. Above all, enjoy yourself!

• *Sunday 2 July* •

You're full of creative ideas today, so give yourself the opportunity to express them. Love is also in the air, and now is the ideal time to tell someone your true feelings. Clear your diary and make sure you've got time to get out and enjoy yourself. A trip to the theatre or cinema would be one way to indulge yourself, especially if you take someone along as a treat.

• Monday 3 July •

Although the weekend may have worn you out, it won't take long to get back into the swing of things and leave your mark on others. Colleagues will find your sense of optimism uplifting, and will expect you to provide some inspiration. You're ready to rise to the challenge and show others what sterling stuff you're made of. This will not go unnoticed, as someone with influence is sure to be impressed by your commitment and determination.

• Tuesday 4 July •

You may want to act impulsively today, especially if people irritate you. Maybe you feel you don't have enough freedom to do what you want, and that people at work are placing too many demands upon you. Not only that, but your ability to get things done is hampered by other people's apparent unwillingness to cooperate with you. Ignore them, and achieve what you can under your own steam.

• Wednesday 5 July •

You may feel as though you are up against the world, as others seem unable or unwilling to understand your motives. Are you sure it's nothing to do with you taking them for granted? Are you pulling your weight at home and at work? If not, you know what you need to do about it. If you are, then you need to stand up for yourself and make sure that others don't take advantage of your good nature.

• Thursday 6 July •

Make sure you find time to indulge yourself today. A shopping spree would do nicely or, even better, a night out dancing with a kindred spirit. You're in the mood for fun and want to share your loving feelings with those to whom you're close. You're also full of creative ideas, so try to find ways of putting them into action. It's the perfect day to fall in love or resolve any problems in your current relationship.

• *Friday 7 July* •

Your mind is full of creative energy at present, so take the opportunity to prepare any work or creative projects that require your full attention. You'll be amazed at how much you can achieve now. The combination of creative ideas and the drive to turn them into reality is fantastic, so don't waste this opportunity. Save some energy to have some fun later on, as you'll be the life and soul of any party. Enjoy yourself!

• *Saturday 8 July* •

You're full of brilliant ideas on improving your position in the world, but under no circumstances allow someone to persuade you to speculate with your money. Although that get-rich-quick scheme may seem foolproof, you can be sure that they're only telling you half the story. Trust your intuition and don't allow yourself to be hoodwinked by someone whose motives may be more suspect than they seem.

• *Sunday 9 July* •

You may feel hypersensitive today, as someone attempts to play on your feelings in order to get their own way. Don't let your sentimentality get the better of you, as it will be better to be strong now even if that makes you seem heartless or unfeeling. The alternative may be to look back and realize that your gullibility has made a fool of you. It is best to walk away from friendships based on manipulation or coercion.

• *Monday 10 July* •

Don't try to make sense of what is going on in your life today as you're sure to get the wrong impression. Although you're feeling confused at present, this feeling will soon pass so don't worry about it. In fact, what will be most helpful now is to get out and have some fun. This will make you realize how true it is that we create our own reality by the way we think about things.

• *Tuesday 11 July* •

You're feeling very grounded today and able to express your thoughts and feelings with affection. This won't be done in a light and flippant way but rather with a serious understanding of the implications of your actions. You'll also want to find structured ways to express your creativity, or maybe you'll just want to visit an art gallery or somewhere else where you can admire people's talents.

• *Wednesday 12 July* •

Don't let anyone at home convince you that your responsibilities lie there rather than at work today. It's a fabulous day for getting things done and impressing others with your industry. People will also value your ability to tune into any undercurrents in the atmosphere, and then soothe the feelings of everyone around you. Don't forget to show the same sensitivity when you return home!

• *Thursday 13 July* •

Over the next few weeks you'll make much more effort than usual to get on well with colleagues and customers. This will stand you in good stead. Right now, you're on the lookout for excitement, or anything else that will give you the chance to express certain parts of your nature that you usually restrain. Others are bound to be shocked, yet they will admire you for your actions, so why hold back?

• *Friday 14 July* •

A day of relative calm beckons, so now is your chance to reflect on recent events in your life and to plan for what lies ahead. You have been full of creative ideas in recent weeks, so take stock of them and consider how you can make them an integral part of your life. Why not join a dance class, for example, or anything else that you've always wanted to do?

• *Saturday 15 July* •

The loving affection you show towards other people ensures that they, in turn, open their hearts to you today. Such feelings are infectious, so you can bet on life at home and at work being like a carnival as you go out of your way to create a party atmosphere. If you're not in a relationship at the moment, romance may beckon, so prepare for action!

• *Sunday 16 July* •

While you have your own views on how to spend the day, other people have very different ideas. There may even be a disagreement with a friend over some social arrangement, and this is bound to make you see red. Today's Full Moon only serves to fan the flames of your anger, as you let this person know in no uncertain terms how disappointed you are by their behaviour. Try to kiss and make up, and remember you're supposed to be enjoying yourself!

• *Monday 17 July* •

A tendency to see a certain person through rose-coloured spectacles could be your downfall today. Could it be that someone at work misinterprets the warmth of your affection for something more than it is? They seem determined to use every trick in the book to play on your sympathy and lead you up the garden path. The problem is that you are, strictly between ourselves, a soft touch right now, so be on your guard.

• Tuesday 18 July •

No one will be more surprised by your sudden actions than you, as swift changes of mood overwhelm you from who knows where. You would like to be helpful to others, yet you have a strong need to spend time alone. You may feel that too much company places heavy demands on your frayed nerves. Don't feel guilty about this. Just make sure that give yourself time to process all the emotions that are currently passing through you.

• Wednesday 19 July •

There are times when the less said, the better, as you will discover today. While you want to reach out to others with warmth and optimism, this is easier said than done now. Either someone criticizes you for not taking life seriously enough, or you sense that this is what they feel about you. This doesn't encourage you to speak your mind spontaneously and may even make you feel like crawling into your shell. Maybe it's their problem, not yours!

• Thursday 20 July •

Get ready for a power struggle when someone seems determined to stand in your way and stop you achieving a certain goal. Don't make a song and dance about it – distract yourself by meeting up with a kindred spirit and having some fun. Even if all you do is have a good old gossip, it's bound to cheer you up.

• Friday 21 July •

Now is the ideal time to make your mark on others and show just how indispensable you are. You're truly inspired today, and if you're at work you can be sure that the ideas you have will win you the respect and admiration of an influential someone. You may also feel strong feelings of love for someone at the moment, and can be sure that they will feel the same. Let's face it, you're simply irresistible!

• *Saturday 22 July* •

If you've got plans to do anything other than go on a shopping spree, then think again. The urge to splurge will prove too great to resist! Apart from that, an exciting day is in prospect, as the warmth of your feelings radiates out and creates a party atmosphere wherever you are. You're also full of good ideas to increase your future earnings, and others will be happy to support your schemes.

• *Sunday 23 July* •

You are full of inspired intuition today and you'll be amazed by the brilliant ideas you come up with. Plans for increasing your income will now be able to take a step forward, and you'll find it difficult to contain your excitement at the prospect. Celebrations are on your mind and you'll want to get out and let your hair down. Make sure that you don't end up spending more than you bargained for!

• *Monday 24 July* •

Difficulties in communicating with others are likely to lead to considerable friction today, especially at work. Maybe you're still suffering from the pleasures of yesterday? Your thinking is so woolly and confused that this is the most likely explanation. The problem is that colleagues are not happy at the thought of having to make allowances for you. Try not to make things worse by reacting badly to their criticism, as they're only doing their job.

• *Tuesday 25 July* •

This is another day in which friction with work colleagues looms on the horizon. It's really up to you to try to make peace, yet you're in no mood to bow to others. In fact, you're likely to feel like giving them a piece of your mind, before storming off in a blaze of glory. Try to bear in mind that this is just a passing phase for you, and that normal service will soon be resumed.

• *Wednesday 26 July* •

Although certain problems may arise in your dealings with others, provided you have been as clear and straightforward as possible, you have no need to worry. The good news is that relationships at work improve, and this will be a big weight off your mind. Try to spend time with loved ones at home. They're sure to spoil you rotten and make you realize how much they care about you.

• *Thursday 27 July* •

Life is very precious to you today, despite all the trials and tribulations that you've had to put up with lately. You're full of compassion and generosity towards others, and will want to go out of your way to offer practical help to someone if it is needed. Family members can also rely on your support now.

• *Friday 28 July* •

Relationships at work and at home are plain sailing today, as others are impressed by the dignified way that you behave with them. Although you're full of confidence, you're also aware of the need to treat others with respect. The favourable effect you have on them ensures that they'll go out of their way to make life pleasant for you. It's all thanks to your positive attitude.

• *Saturday 29 July* •

Your emotional responses will be unpredictable to say the least today, as you find yourself in the grip of sudden impulses. Perhaps you feel a strong attraction for someone at work, even though you've never thought about them in that way in the past? Or maybe someone you casually meet creates a flutter in your heart that you'd never have believed possible. Such things can happen, and usually when least expected!

• *Sunday 30 July* •

You want to find constructive ways to express your creativity today. In fact, you'll be driven to do so, as your energy is too restless to be contained unless you find a practical outlet for it. You may also want to write to someone you care about, and now would be a good time, as you're able to say what you mean. Someone needs your help and you won't think twice before rushing to assist.

• *Monday 31 July* •

If important discussions or negotiations need to take place, don't waste today's opportunity to get the ball rolling. You're feeling resourceful, creative and able to see the game plan. You can also deal well with people in established positions of authority, and they'll recognize your skills. It's a good time to seek a pay rise or to apply for a more senior position, but make sure you don't come across as too self-willed.

AUGUST AT A GLANCE

Love	♥ ♥ ♥ ♥ ♥
Money	£
Career	💻 💻 💻 💻 💻
Health	☼ ☼ ☼ ☼ ☼

• *Tuesday 1 August* •

Although you can expect your work performance to increase dramatically over the next six weeks, today may bring a temporary hiccup. While you're more concerned with your colleagues and your relationships with them, others may accuse you of gossiping or taking things easy. Expect a few unpleasant comments about this, but don't let that stop you from doing what you know is right.

• *Wednesday 2 August* •

Your willpower and resourcefulness ensure a successful day, so make your move if you want to impress someone with your command of a situation. People at work will be amazed by your actions, as they realize what an asset you are. This is a time to act boldly and to fulfil your ambitions. You can be sure that anyone influential will support you because they can recognize your sterling qualities.

• *Thursday 3 August* •

Don't hesitate to tell someone how much you feel for them today. You can trust your feelings and will be able to say exactly what you mean without dressing it up in flowery language. Colleagues at work prove helpful in advising you how to deal with a certain financial matter that needs resolving. A productive day is in store, so take full advantage of it.

● *Friday 4 August* ●

Trust your hunches today, as your understanding of any situation in which you find yourself will be crystal clear. It's an excellent time to resolve any financial matters, especially if they involve other people. Workmates will be cooperative and will go out of their way to show their respect for you. For your part, you'll want to help a certain person who is currently in trouble.

● *Saturday 5 August* ●

Someone may try to use all their wiles to make you part with your money today, but you're far too canny to fall for their tricks. Your insights could astonish you but be sure to trust them because they could get you out of a jam. A colleague at work asks you for advice, as they know they can trust you with their secret. This will strengthen your relationship in the weeks to come.

● *Sunday 6 August* ●

You could hear something that makes you sad or disappointed today. It couldn't arrive at a worse time. You're feeling particularly sensitive and would prefer to give bad news a wide berth if you could. Be choosy about whose shoulder you cry on because certain people will be surprisingly unsympathetic and only make you feel worse than you did originally. It's best to keep your own company now.

● *Monday 7 August* ●

You're ready to make contact with the world again, and will want to bring a light touch to all your communications. Not too much, however, as you've got serious matters to discuss. Today finds you feeling realistic and well organized, and also able to concentrate on your work. If you've been putting off any major tasks involving mental discipline, then now is the time to tackle them.

• Tuesday 8 August •

Expect to find yourself in the doldrums today as your energy starts to flag. You need to focus on being realistic and practical at work, but this could be easier said than done as you're unable to immerse yourself in what's happening around you. Be aware of what you say and do because some actions could be well-meaning but misguided. You should also take care of your health today as you aren't feeling as strong as usual.

• Wednesday 9 August •

Your ability to function at work or in your daily routines is affected by your woolly state of mind today. Because you're in a daydream, you're likely to be absent-minded, and this will interfere with your commitments to others. You may even consider resorting to deliberate deception in order to cover up for your forgetfulness, but this will only make the situation worse. Try to be attentive, even though that may be difficult.

• Thursday 10 August •

You now have the opportunity to make up for time lost over the last two days. Your mind is alert, and you have the energy and determination to get on with your work. You'll be astounded at how much you can achieve as you plough through the backlog. Because you're in overdrive, watch out for impulsive behaviour and try not to fly off the handle with colleagues who struggle to keep up with you.

• Friday 11 August •

You're full of brilliant ideas today and able to win the support of other people. However, make sure that you win their cooperation before you put these ideas into practice. You have a strong need to do things your way without any kind of interference. Take care that you don't alienate anyone who might otherwise help you by acting in an impulsive and rash manner.

• *Saturday 12 August* •

You are in a very focused state today, and capable of looking beneath the surface to what is really going on. This will help you to achieve great things, especially at work, so be prepared for lots of compliments and pats on the back. If any task has seemed beyond your capacity recently, now is the time to have another go at it. You could find that you polish it off in no time at all.

• *Sunday 13 August* •

You feel torn between the urge to indulge yourself and the need to get on with some jobs around the house. Why not do both? There's plenty of time to do some work and also to enjoy yourself, especially with a loved one who will thrive on your attention. Watch out, though, for a tendency to over-indulge yourself, as you may regret it later on.

• *Monday 14 August* •

Someone you thought you could trust wants to stab you in the back and you're mystified why they should want to do this. Whether it's someone at work or a close partner is unclear. The question is, have you been honest in your dealings with them? If not, then you shouldn't be surprised by their actions now. If you have been straight with them, then consider whether their current behaviour is because they are feeling insecure or jealous.

• *Tuesday 15 August* •

Today's Full Moon highlights issues connected with your health and work over the coming fortnight. You may feel under the weather and the chances are that stress is the cause of it, so try to find some time to relax. Maybe now is a good chance to look more generally at ways in which you can improve your health through your diet, and perhaps also take more exercise. Watch out at work for friction caused by crossed wires.

• *Wednesday 16 August* •

You can achieve great things today because your energy and willpower will enable you to move mountains. You'll make great progress in your work and will win the admiration of whoever you want to impress. One thing to watch out for is a tendency to push your ideas down other people's throats. This will work against you and may even mean that you lose someone's support.

• *Thursday 17 August* •

After yesterday's exertions, a day of relative calm seems on the cards. Now is the time to take stock of recent events and work out your future strategies. If you haven't had the time recently, you could now check out the local sports centre and decide what sort of exercise would suit you best. Sometimes life is so frantic that we forget that we need to look after ourselves.

• *Friday 18 August* •

Take note of any ideas you have for increasing your income today, especially if they are connected with your plans for the future. You also want to spend money on your home, and the more luxurious the items, the happier you will be. Not that you'll go mad, as you're aware of the need to balance your books right now. Life at home today promises both joy and stability. Enjoy it.

• *Saturday 19 August* •

You're full of energy, and your ability to achieve important goals ensures that no task will be too great for you now. What's more, other people will be only too happy to help you if they can, so don't be afraid to ask for assistance if you need it. Don't expect everything to go to plan, however, as lots of sudden and exciting events will distract you, but they'll be great fun and might even make your day.

• *Sunday 20 August* •

You could happily while away the day in casual chatter, enjoying the company of others. This wouldn't be such a bad thing as we all need to wind down at times. However, the urge to get on with numerous routine chores that have fallen by the wayside recently may prove irresistible. You'll feel happy about whatever you do, as you're at peace with yourself. Don't let anyone else's negativity get you down.

• *Monday 21 August* •

Watch out that your sharp tongue doesn't get you into a mess today. You're feeling quite tense and irritable, especially if you're at work, and it won't take much for you to explode into rage. If someone annoys you, try counting to ten before you respond. Similarly, take care when driving, because there's a chance you could have an accident caused by acting too impulsively. Other people will be unable to predict your behaviour.

• *Tuesday 22 August* •

A sense of gnawing frustration remains with you throughout the day, as you seek to make things happen even though the time is not yet ripe for them. Work is the most likely arena, and you'll be full of plans for things you want to achieve right now. Unfortunately, your ideas don't always go to plan and communication problems could create a major difficulty for you. Rather than losing your temper with everyone, you may as well bow to the inevitable.

• Wednesday 23 August •

It's another day of feeling thwarted in your attempts to get on with things. This time, though, it looks as if someone is deliberately trying to scupper your plans and make things as difficult as possible. Maybe they're fed up with your recent irritability and want to give you a taste of your own medicine. Or perhaps they want you to realize that you're not the most important person in the world. Take a back seat and think whether they're right.

• Thursday 24 August •

You're full of brilliant ideas for making changes to your home, and there's no doubt that you're truly inspired today. However, don't make the mistake of putting your ideas into action until you've discussed them with your partner or the rest of the family. If you do go ahead without their say-so, they'll feel angry about not being involved in the decision, even though they'll probably love your plans. Life is too short for dramas that can be avoided.

• Friday 25 August •

Make sure you set some time aside for fun and frivolity today, as you're definitely in the mood for them. If you're in a relationship, now is the time to breathe some new life into it. If you're single, you might woo someone new into your life. Don't stay at home in front of the TV – get out and mingle if possible.

• *Saturday 26 August* •

Is that a twinkle in your eye? You feel cheerful and affectionate, and see the world for the beautiful place that it is. Your responsiveness to beauty gives you a radiance that attracts others like bees to honey. Don't waste this opportunity by staying at home. Get out and enjoy yourself – dancing would be perfect, but any kind of social event will be good, if you're feeling up to it.

• *Sunday 27 August* •

High drama looks inevitable today when a partner takes you to task over recent behaviour. Could it be that you've spent too little time at home and too much at work, or are there deeper issues involved? One thing for certain is that they're going to make a meal of it. Some of their accusations may seem quite outrageous, but they're based on their very deep and hurt feelings. Ignore these at your peril.

• *Monday 28 August* •

Take great care if you're at work today, as your energy level is so high that you could end up going through the roof. No task will prove too demanding for you, other than that of trying to cooperate with others! While you're sure that you're the only person who's up to the job in hand, others may disagree. This could easily lead to a dispute that gets completely out of control.

• *Tuesday 29 August* •

You're so determined to brook no interference from colleagues today that you risk alienating yourself from them. What's more, you may be so obsessed with your right to do your own thing that you end up making a big scene. Think carefully, as you may not have the opportunity to undo any damage that you do now. Also, take care not to act out your anger from work on a partner. They will not be amused.

• *Wednesday 30 August* •

After the extraordinary events of the past two days, you now have the opportunity to think about the implications of your actions. If you've been foolhardy, you're probably now wondering what on earth got into you. You'll have an opportunity to put things right with your partner tomorrow, so consider if that's what you want, and then plan accordingly.

• *Thursday 31 August* •

Fortune is on your side today, as you now have the chance to make amends for recent events. What's more, if your relationship has hit the rocks, your partner will realize now that you're serious about making it up to them. Your sense of responsibility, as well as your genuine affection, will be quite apparent. This should prove sufficient commitment to ensure that your relationship returns to a more stable footing.

SEPTEMBER AT A GLANCE

Love	♥ ♥ ♥ ♥ ♥
Money	£ $ £ $ £
Career	💻 💻
Health	☼ ☼ ☼

• *Friday 1 September* •

Your ability to look beneath the surface of things to discover what is really going on is quite uncanny today. Any complicated financial matters that you're embroiled in can be tackled, as you're now able to find solutions where there were only problems previously. You're also able to help sort out a tricky situation at work. Colleagues will be amazed by your determination to persevere with the task until you have succeeded.

• *Saturday 2 September* •

Either you or a close partner seem particularly self-righteous and determined to be in control today. If it's you, take a long hard look at what you expect to gain from forcing your views on others. The only thing you're guaranteed is disruption, both at home and at work. The chances are that you'll also lose the respect of those who previously looked up to you. Is it worth it?

• *Sunday 3 September* •

If you've ever ridiculed those who talk of psychic sensitivity, then you may now have to eat your words. You might have inspired ideas out of the blue concerning all manner of things. Not only this, but your capacity to get to the bottom of things will startle you into looking at the world in a completely new way. You can also expect to feel much more sensitive and loving towards others right now.

• *Monday 4 September* •

You may want to force your ideas upon other people now but this will simply alienate you from them. You may also seek to point out their failings to them without being aware of your own. Whoops! Family members, or people you work with, will be quick to pick up on your double standards. You may also overreach yourself because you have an inflated belief in your abilities, and this could mean you come a cropper. Think carefully!

• Tuesday 5 September •

If you haven't learned your lesson from yesterday, you can expect a bundle of problems today as other people make it quite clear they won't be bullied by you. Although you're desperate to reach your goals and glory in your achievements, is it worth walking over other people in order to attain them? Fame and success are all very well, but they come with a hefty price tag today.

• Wednesday 6 September •

If you managed to control yourself yesterday, today will bring you the reward. You're now able to make your move to show others just how dynamic you are, as well as reminding them that you are an indispensable member of the team. Whatever tasks you set yourself can be achieved easily, as others will be happy to lend a helping hand. They'll also be fascinated by your current insight and inventiveness.

• Thursday 7 September •

All you want is to enjoy yourself today and do as little as possible. Unfortunately, you're also unduly sensitive and are likely to take offence when none is intended. Your failed attempts to persuade a friend to join your plans for the day leave you feeling hurt and unloved. Maybe the simple fact is that they can't afford to keep up with you, but they're too proud to say so. Dig deep into your pocket if it's that important.

• Friday 8 September •

Set your sights high, as little is beyond your capacity today. You're feeling truly inspired because you know that your hunches are bang on the nail. Any business plans you have are certain to win the approval of others, as they can see that you know what you're talking about. Property matters may prove lucrative. Set aside some time to enjoy the company of loved ones at home.

• *Saturday 9 September* •

You could feel like a psychic sponge today as you absorb the feelings of everyone around you. What's more, you're also feeling particularly compassionate and will want to help a certain person within your family who's going through a hard time. You may even give them a loan or donation if you can afford it.

• *Sunday 10 September* •

Have you ever considered a technique called creative visualization? This is nothing more than mind over matter, and you might find that you're rather good at it today. Your current ability to tune into your intuition is phenomenal, and enables you to understand much about yourself and others that was previously hidden. Take this precious opportunity to think deeply about where your life is heading. You will also have a great chance to resolve any outstanding financial matters that have troubled you recently.

• *Monday 11 September* •

Sudden changes of mood that you can't explain may make you feel irritable and unable to cope with other people today. While you might have lots of exciting ideas, these won't help you to deal with the mundane matters of the day. Colleagues at work will prove unsympathetic to your state of mind, and you'll have to muster all your self-control to avoid a major fall-out. Try not to react to their anger.

• *Tuesday 12 September* •

You may feel that it's you against the world today, as others seem hell-bent on thwarting you at every turn. The question is, are you fulfilling all your responsibilities and acting as honestly as you should? If not, don't be surprised if family members or people at work take you to task. Although you're sensitive to criticism right now, you'd do well to listen to what you are told. It will be painful but pertinent.

• *Wednesday 13 September* •

Today's Full Moon highlights close personal relationships, so this is the area to focus on over the coming fortnight. You may find that a certain person thinks you aren't paying them enough attention. Make an effort to reassure them that they're still the most important thing in the world to you, or prepare for high drama. Fortunately, you're sensitive enough to put their mind at rest.

• *Thursday 14 September* •

An exciting day beckons on almost every front today. Your business acumen will astound others as you show just how penetrating your mind can be when you apply it in earnest. Any matters relating to your work, joint financial matters or property will be easily resolved by your scintillating vision, so get your brain in gear. Love is also on the menu, so prepare for an opportunity to indulge your favourite dish!

• *Friday 15 September* •

Ideas you have for improving your financial situation will propel you into action now. You're ready to make your mark on the world, and a certain person will go out of their way to help. It's not all plain sailing though, as someone with a vested interest seems determined to try to spoil your plans. Don't worry, because you're full of brilliant ideas and will be sure to outmanoeuvre this person when push comes to shove.

• *Saturday 16 September* •

A further opportunity arises to push ahead your plans, and there's no way you're going to miss out on it. Colleagues will be only too happy to support you, because they know that the action you're taking is constructive and that it will help them in the long run as well. They also know that your direct approach is a reflection of your honesty, and they can therefore trust you. Now is the time for action!

• *Sunday 17 September* •

In complete contrast to yesterday's expansive mood, you're now feeling reclusive and full of self-doubt. Your ability to communicate with others is affected, and you'd do well to spend as much time on your own as possible. At least this will minimize the amount of confusion you experience with others, as you're sure to misunderstand what they tell you now. Try to find some time for peaceful reflection, as this will help.

• *Monday 18 September* •

Have you ever felt as though you are driving with the brakes on? That's how you'll feel today as you desperately seek to get on with things, only to find yourself stopped in your tracks. Is it a close partner or family member who seems determined to thwart you, or is it simply that you haven't prepared the ground before embarking on your current project? Find some demanding task that will enable you to burn off your frustration.

• *Tuesday 19 September* •

Don't waste any opportunity to get your brain into gear today. Your mind is simply brilliant, and will be able to untangle any problem you meet. You're also uncannily aware of things going on beneath the surface and will be able to read people's motives like an open book. If you have to make any financial decisions involving others, then you can be sure to trust your hunches. Don't let anyone change your mind.

• *Wednesday 20 September* •

Family life provides a constant source of excitement now as unexpected comings and going enrich your day. Maybe you'll come up with some fantastic plans for changing your home, or even consider plans to up sticks. If so, you can be sure that it will be a smart move, as you can trust your financial judgement. What's more, a certain family member will be only too happy to help you out if needed.

• *Thursday 21 September* •

What happened to yesterday's sense of goodwill? Could it be that you've been merrily making plans without consulting someone who should be involved? If so, you can be sure that they'll let you know exactly what they think. Take it on the chin and then get on with the job of talking them round to your way of seeing things. It's an excellent day to sort out all routine work as your focus is as sharp as a razor.

• *Friday 22 September* •

Don't let anyone persuade you into parting with your cash over some half-baked get-rich-quick scheme today. You may find yourself feeling quite irritable, and lovers as well as children will feel the edge of your tongue as they push your buttons without even realizing it. It's not a good day to share a secret with someone. They might accidentally blurt it out and you'll get the blame for it.

• *Saturday 23 September* •

This is the perfect day to resolve any complicated financial wrangling in which you've recently been engaged. All the more so if the matter concerns property or if it involves anyone within your family. You can act constructively and with a sense of responsibility that is sure to win the confidence of others. People who are able to help you will gladly step forward, because they know you can be trusted.

• *Sunday 24 September* •

While your focus is on how you can increase your general efficiency, you should also consider how you can ensure that your broader vision doesn't get lost in the clutter of daily life. You're at risk of fraying your nerves through being too pre-occupied with anxieties that you can't do much about, so why not step back today and stop worrying. Let tomorrow take care of itself, in its own time.

• *Monday 25 September* •

Try to nip emotional problems in the bud and express your feelings to a close partner who is feeling unloved and un-wanted at the moment. If you don't, words that remain unspoken will take on a life of their own, and you'll regret your failure to put someone's worries at bay. They might release the tension by starting a row or nagging at you, and that won't exactly be a picnic.

• *Tuesday 26 September* •

Your sensitivity and feelings for others are as boundless as the ocean today, and you'll go out of your way to help someone in need. If this happens to involve digging deep into your pocket, then so be it. You'll have no regrets about parting with your cash, even though you know you'll never see it again. This is because you realize that there's more to life than how much money you have.

• *Wednesday 27 September* •

Don't bother trying to make sense of the world today. You're full of dreams and looking at everything through rose-coloured spectacles. Be careful about making commitments to anyone, as they may be playing on your sympathy and you cannot guarantee sufficient resources to help out. While your willingness to see the best in everyone is an excellent quality, don't let this prevent you from viewing things as they really are.

• *Thursday 28 September* •

Nothing will amaze you today as much as the uncanny brilliance of your hunches, as you astound others with your ability to pinpoint exactly what's going on. It's a time when everything you touch turns to gold, so take advantage of the opportunity to sort out any financial matters that have been hanging fire recently. There might also be a good opportunity on the domestic front.

• *Friday 29 September* •

This is an excellent day to make contact with someone who now lives far away. They'll be delighted to hear from you and there'll be no shortage of things to talk about. You might also start thinking about doing a course in higher education for which you've never had the time previously. If you've got in-laws, you may want to help them out today, but make sure they need your assistance before you offer it.

• Saturday 30 September •

Today finds you pondering on the meaning of life and willing to share your views with anyone who cares to listen. Your far-sighted thoughts may even lead you in the direction of the nearest travel agent, as the images of exotic lands prove irresistible. You have such a strong yearning to be free now that you may be tempted to make a booking on the spot. However, perhaps you should wait until you're feeling less excitable and impulsive?

OCTOBER AT A GLANCE

Love	♥ ♥ ♥ ♥
Money	£ $ £ $
Career	💻 💻 💻 💻 💻
Health	☼ ☼

• Sunday 1 October •

This is not the best of times to focus your mind on practical matters because you're prone to daydream, making you vague and confused when talking to others. It also means that your attention span is not up to coping with the stress of normal activity. You'll enjoy planning a foreign holiday or discussing subjects like philosophy or religion. Your mind can then wander free of restraint without having to operate in a structured way.

• Monday 2 October •

Romance is in the air because you're feeling a sense of inner harmony and will express this in your dealings with others. If you're in a relationship, explore ways in which you can continue to grow together through your mutual interests or understanding. If you're single, now is the time to explore fresh pastures in search of love and adventure. It's also a time when you're feeling very creative, so try to find some way to express it.

• Tuesday 3 October •

Can you keep your head when everyone else is losing their cool? Either a close partner or someone who has some degree of power over you loses their rag and becomes decidedly unpleasant today. While it would be easy to react to their rage, will it get you anywhere? Try to stand back from this person and defuse their negativity by not responding to it. You'll be amazed at the results.

• Wednesday 4 October •

If you're thinking of buying or selling your home, now is the perfect time to act. Your belief in what you're doing ensures that you'll make the right decision, as well as encouraging others to give you any assistance you might need. Make sure your partner or family is on your side, as they won't take kindly to being told of your activity after the event. Make plans for an exciting night with them!

• Thursday 5 October •

It looks as though some straight talking is needed, because a certain person wants to take advantage of your good nature. Or is it the other way round? Observe your behaviour and make sure you're not the guilty party. Once this matter is resolved, you have the opportunity to strengthen this friendship by being open with each other. Indeed, it's only when a relationship survives a trauma or fall-out that you can know its strength.

• *Friday 6 October* •

There are times when a family is worth its weight in gold, and this is one of them. While you're feeling sensitive and keen to withdraw from others, you can be sure that someone at home understands your plight. They'll do everything they can to make you feel that home is truly where the heart is. This is a time to retire from the hustle and bustle, put your feet up, and relax. Bliss!

• *Saturday 7 October* •

You could feel extremely sensitive today and will want to play the role of saviour to anyone who needs to be bailed out. You're also full of ideas to improve various aspects of your life, especially concerning your work. Life at home is sure to be a bundle of fun, as you're feeling so positive. One thing to watch for is getting involved in an argument with a member of the clan, especially if they belong to your partner's branch of the family.

• *Sunday 8 October* •

You're in the mood for love today, and the more mysterious or unusual it is, the better. You could be fascinated by someone from another country or culture, because you're currently attracted to anything that is new and different. If you already have a partner, make a point of planning something exciting or completely wacky with them, in order to breathe new fire into your ardour.

• *Monday 9 October* •

After yesterday's glamour and excitement, prepare to fall back to the ground with a crash. What goes up must come down, and now you're left wondering where all the magic has gone. Try not to let your sense of melancholy drag you down as you're not in the mood to get yourself back on an even keel today. Trying to communicate with others will only make you feel worse, so don't look to them for salvation.

• *Tuesday 10 October* •

Like a yo-yo, you're back on your feet, ready for anything and everything today. You want to express your originality and creativity because you're positively brimming with things that you want to say and do. You're also incredibly intuitive, and will be fully aware of everything that is going on around you. People's motives will be crystal clear to you, and this gives you the edge in any financial dealings you're currently involved in.

• *Wednesday 11 October* •

Your affectionate nature is sure to rub off on others today and help you to put across your ideas in a discussion or negotiation, particularly if this is connected with education or something with global overtones. Your home life feels settled and you may also have some practical ideas for improving your domestic situation. Don't be afraid to act on them.

• *Thursday 12 October* •

Hunches that come out of the blue will amaze you today. They prove how resourceful you can be when you put your mind to it. Be sure to take the opportunity to express your views to someone with the power to act on them, as they're sure to be impressed by your grasp of the situation. The confidence this will give you can only make you feel more positive, and will guarantee your future happiness.

• *Friday 13 October* •

Conflict is in the air, so try to avoid falling out with someone. This is not the time to get involved in any financial discussions. You can be sure that others will be obstructive just for the hell of it. However, avoid taking the high moral ground either at home or at work, as you may get carried away by your own opinions. This will lead to serious disagreements, so try to keep any homilies to yourself.

• *Saturday 14 October* •

No matter how hard you try to work out what is going on, you'll still get the wrong end of the stick today. That might be because certain people are deliberately trying to deceive you, or because you are feeling confused or unsure of yourself. Perhaps you're in such a daydream that your uncontrolled imagination distorts what's actually going on, so you pick up the wrong impressions. Take care!

• *Sunday 15 October* •

This is another day in which you need to be careful about how you communicate with others. After yesterday's difficulties you feel frustrated, and this is likely to come out in your dealings with other people. Someone that you thought might understand what you are going through could turn out to be surprisingly unsympathetic or dismissive.

• *Monday 16 October* •

You're aware of the need to be completely practical and down-to-earth in the way you relate to others today. However, this awareness will not exactly cheer you up and may, in fact, make you feel quite negative and depressed for a while. Never mind, because you will hear some good news that soon has you back on top form. You may also want to help someone in need.

• *Tuesday 17 October* •

You're full of optimistic and brilliant ideas for improving things at home today, yet a close partner sees things from a different point of view and may even block your progress. You may also encounter opposition from someone whose support you need. There's no point in flogging a dead horse by trying to get them to change their mind today. Give them time, and they may come round to your way of thinking.

• Wednesday 18 October •

Now is the ideal time to sit down with someone and sort out your financial situation. Whatever plans you present will be well received, as they will be impressed by your honesty, and your sunny disposition will soon charm them into submission. Anything to do with your home or property in general will go well, whether you are buying something minor or planning a massive investment.

• Thursday 19 October •

Difficulties in communications leave you feeling lonely and disappointed today. You will take everything very personally and may feel that things have gone wrong because others don't care enough about you. This is especially likely if you are involved in a close relationship that is currently going through the doldrums. Try to recapture your sense of humour, otherwise you will feel increasingly wretched.

• Friday 20 October •

Children or loved ones will seek to empty your pockets today because they want you to pay for their entertainment. Although you'll resent their selfishness at the time, your loving nature will eventually get the better of you, as you can't bear the thought of seeing them so miserable! Confusion at work looks likely, so try not to get too caught up in other people's problems. Misplaced sympathy may result in your workload getting out of control.

• *Saturday 21 October* •

You are all set for a happy time on the domestic front when your good humour pays dividends. There's also a great opportunity to stake your claim for more money or responsibility at work, when you prove your abilities to others. Don't bite off more than you can chew, though, by making unexpected or unreasonable demands on others.

• *Sunday 22 October* •

You can feel great sympathy for others today. You're intuitively aware of how they're feeling and will want to help them if possible. You're also feeling inspired by all sorts of creative ideas that will help you to achieve your current goals, especially if you're involved in any artistic activities. You may also have a hankering to live a more fulfilling or spiritual life. If so, how can you go about it?

• *Monday 23 October* •

Trying to balance your commitments at work with your responsibilities at home will mean that you have your hands full today. Whichever way you approach the situation, someone is going to have a go at you. Although a certain family member will feel deflated by your inability to stick to a previous plan, this is a better option for you than facing the fury of someone at work.

• *Tuesday 24 October* •

Think carefully about how you come across to other people today. You have the ability and patience to see the broad picture and to work towards your goals with the support of others. However, if you try to push things along too forcefully, you'll meet incredible resistance from people who would normally want to help you. Use your skill to win them over with gentle persuasion, rather than relying on brute force.

• *Wednesday 25 October* •

Any issues requiring an ability to see beneath the surface of things are easily tackled today. Your intuition is faultless and enables you to know exactly what to say or do in order to achieve your goals. What's more, colleagues or family will want to go out of their way to help, because they appreciate that you know what you're doing. Trust your hunches, even if that means taking a risk.

• *Thursday 26 October* •

Try to step back from the world today in order to look at what is really going on. Your sense of direction is obscured by your inability to concentrate at the moment, because you're in such a dreamy state. This is all very well if you have the time for meditation or some kind of creative work. However, it could be a struggle to focus on everyday activities or things that require a cool head and an eye for detail.

• *Friday 27 October* •

Don't be surprised if you find yourself preoccupied with dreams of foreign travel today, or perhaps you'll hear from someone who lives abroad. Try not to let this distract you from your responsibilities at home or at work, because you'll grab any opportunity to take things easy! All you really want to do is indulge yourself in as extravagant a manner as possible. Fulfil your obligations first, and then you can have a good time with a clear conscience.

• *Saturday 28 October* •

Today presents the perfect opportunity to achieve your wildest dreams, as you reach for the sky. You exude a magnetic presence which others are sure to pick up on, while still leaving them like putty in your hands. A romantic opportunity might arise at work or your charm may enable you to further your ambitions, thanks to someone's admiration for you. Your emotions are intense today, so make sure you express them.

• *Sunday 29 October* •

Loved ones aren't very happy with you today because other commitments are keeping you apart. Although this will make you feel miserable, the achievements that you make will more than make up for your low mood. The fact is that even if you stayed at home someone would make life uncomfortable for you. As it is, your uncanny perceptions ensure that you can move a certain ambition at least one step closer to being realized.

• *Monday 30 October* •

Your thoughts take a very adventurous turn today, and you may be preoccupied with new ways of making sense of what your life is all about. This may include planning your next holiday or even considering taking some further education. You're also ready to stake your claim in order to achieve a certain ambition, and your sense of timing is perfect. Charm will open many doors for you now.

• *Tuesday 31 October* •

Don't expect a close partner to be too happy with your antics today, as they seem convinced that you think your work is more important than your relationship. They're not going to take this lying down, so prepare yourself for a major drama. Alternatively, someone at work whose cooperation you rely upon proves that they're not worthy of your trust. Giving them a piece of your mind is what they deserve, but dare you do it?

NOVEMBER AT A GLANCE

Love	♥ ♥ ♥ ♥
Money	£ $ £ $
Career	💻 💻 💻 💻 💻
Health	☼ ☼

• Wednesday 1 November •

Trying to make sense of things may prove difficult today. The problem is that your mind is everywhere except where it's supposed to be! You may find yourself dreaming of beautiful foreign locations or contemplating the meaning of life. This is all very well, provided others aren't reliant upon your ability to function now. Communications with others will be confusing, but make sure you're not the guilty party.

• Thursday 2 November •

Unusual and unexpected opportunities enable you to move forward with plans which will improve your business or career. This is because you're open to other people's ideas and that will go down very well with them. This is also true in your close relationships, and someone will respond to your intention to be more open when dealing with them. This is a very positive time because you'll be able to resolve any outstanding issues between you.

• Friday 3 November •

A certain friend proves their weight in gold, thanks to the advice they give you today. Their ideas will give you lots to think about and will prove particularly helpful in dealing with a close partner. Although someone makes a biting remark to you or accuses you of living in a dream, you're far too well meaning to react to their anger. In fact, your tactic of killing them with kindness leaves them defenceless!

• *Saturday 4 November* •

Although you got off the hook yesterday, someone seems determined to annoy you again and prove that you're human after all. What they won't expect is the startling and unusual way in which you respond to them. You're feeling far too warm and affectionate to lose your cool, although you won't lose the opportunity to show this person how ridiculous their behaviour is. However, don't expect any thanks for this.

• *Sunday 5 November* •

Try not to carry the weight of the world on your shoulders today. Life is far too short for that and it won't do you or anyone else any good. Trying to communicate with others will prove difficult right now. You feel isolated and unloved at the moment, so this makes it difficult for others to breach your defences. However, you will hear something that cheers you up.

• *Monday 6 November* •

Although you feel positive and believe that all things are possible today, others will try to undermine your confidence now. Family members will not take kindly to your assumption that you're free to do as you please. Similarly, someone with authority is determined to place some controls on you and make you more accountable to them. Don't pick an argument over this issue at the moment as you're in no position to win.

• *Tuesday 7 November* •

Your sensitivity towards others and your sunny nature opens the hearts of those around you today. You're feeling very philosophical and want to share your ideas with everyone you come across. You will also enjoy doing some mental or physical travelling, especially if you can discover more about the world in the process. Whatever you do now will reflect your positive outlook.

• *Wednesday 8 November* •

You're brimming with ideas about how to increase your income or make positive changes at home. Quite where the ideas are coming from is a mystery, as they seem to come out of the blue. One thing for sure is that they'll meet resistance from someone who feels they should have a piece of the action. Try to reassure them that anything good for you should be good for them as well.

• *Thursday 9 November* •

You feel as if someone's given you an electric shock when energy ripples through you in a dramatic fashion. This makes you feel quite impulsive, and you could react to others in erratic ways. Anything that challenges your need to feel free will whip you up into an excitable state. You'll find it difficult to understand your reactions, so you can imagine how mystified everyone else will feel!

• *Friday 10 November* •

If you need to sort out some financial affairs with other people, try to do it today. Your hunches and instincts will allow you to find solutions where previously there were only problems. On top of that, you're able to tune into others and persuade them to see your side of things. Because you're feeling so sensitive you'll want to help someone else out, even if it means being out of pocket as a result.

• *Saturday 11 November* •

Today's Full Moon will highlight your communications over the coming fortnight. You could hear something that produces a strong emotional reaction in you. Check your facts before you say anything you might regret at a later date. Consider this carefully because you're feeling particularly impulsive and are likely to react without thinking first.

• *Sunday 12 November* •

After yesterday's intensity, you're feeling far more tentative in the way you communicate with others. This is partly because you're feeling quite low, but also because you half expect to get your head bitten off by someone who is breathing fire. Relax, and try to enjoy the day at home with those who care about you. The atmosphere here will soothe your frayed nerves, revitalize you and remind you about what really matters to you.

• *Monday 13 November* •

Work is the last place in the world you'll want to be today. You'd much rather be at home, surrounded by your nearest and dearest. Be careful that you don't allow your good feelings to dissolve into negativity towards your colleagues at work. They'll be sure to resent it, and this will bounce back against you in a way that could affect you profoundly.

• *Tuesday 14 November* •

As with yesterday, you'll feel a strong pull between work and home. Sacrifices have to be made and there's little point in responding negatively to other people's demands upon you. You're extra sensitive today and will take even the slightest criticism to heart, so try to bear this in mind. On a positive note, you're full of good ideas for ways of resolving any outstanding financial matters, especially if they relate to your present home.

• *Wednesday 15 November* •

Take care not to misunderstand something you're told today. News from abroad or from members of the family leaves you distinctly confused about what's going on. Don't try to make sense of it right now without hearing it from the horse's mouth. No matter how hard you try, you're likely to distort what you're told and that won't help to straighten things out.

• *Thursday 16 November* •

An exciting day is on the cards as your confidence, enthusiasm and love of adventure are all working well. If any financial deals are on the agenda, this is a good day to get on with them. You're sure to get everyone involved in your plans because your drive to succeed is irrepressible. It's also the ideal time to start any home improvement projects you've been thinking about. Make sure you also get out and have some fun at some point.

• *Friday 17 November* •

After yesterday's exertions, you are probably feeling tired, worn out and slightly irritable. Try not to take this out on your colleagues because they want to help you if possible. They may even enable you to achieve something totally unexpected, and this will raise your standing with people you hope to impress. If there are deals to be done, you're definitely up for it. You'll also enjoy any time spent at home.

• *Saturday 18 November* •

Try to avoid work situations whenever possible today. It's one of those days when all kinds of little things go wrong, leaving you with a sense of seething irritability. Wires could get crossed and colleagues may be unhelpful. No matter how hard you try, it will be a struggle to stay cool. You may also be feeling under the weather, and this will hardly improve your state of mind.

• *Sunday 19 November* •

No matter how hard you try to convey exactly what you want to say today, others will apparently go out of their way to misunderstand you. What's more, they'll provoke you by trying to impose heavy demands on you. Apart from the fact that you don't have the energy for all this, you'll also resent other people acting in an authoritarian manner towards you. Make sure you don't behave in the same way yourself.

• *Monday 20 November* •

Although the working week begins here, make sure you spend some time with a loved one. Not only will your loving feelings be well received, this is an excellent time to discuss any issues that need to be raised. You can talk things through constructively. What's more, because you're both feeling safe with each other, there's little chance of any misunderstandings. Terrific!

• *Tuesday 21 November* •

Passions run deep today and your energy is almost unbounded. You'll need to find ways to express it, because otherwise you're likely to explode in anger. The chances are that it will be a close partner or a good friend who's on the receiving end of your ire. If you're angry, let it out immediately, otherwise your feelings will stew and then erupt uncontrollably. Even so, a great day lies in store, and you'll be delighted with what you accomplish.

• *Wednesday 22 November* •

Prepare for another day in which your passions are on the rampage! Your feelings for a certain person are very strong, but are they reciprocated? If they're not, you may feel rejected. You're particularly prone to feeling jealous at the moment and are liable to fly off the handle without a second's hesitation. Arguments with a friend over a joint financial matter are also likely, so try to avoid talking about it at the moment.

• *Thursday 23 November* •

Other people may find it difficult to get through to you today. Your mind is wandering everywhere except where it's supposed to be. That means it's a wonderful day to relax, perhaps by taking a gentle stroll or visiting somewhere very restful. It's also a good opportunity to start making plans for Christmas, especially if you're beginning to glance nervously at the calendar and are wondering how you will get everything done in time.

• *Friday 24 November* •

After yesterday's mental meandering, you're ready to take the world by storm today. Your energy is phenomenal and you know exactly what you want to achieve. Nothing will escape your scrutiny, as your intuition ensures that you'll know exactly what is going on around you. It's an excellent day for any financial ventures in which you're involved. You also have the opportunity to impress a powerful person who can open new doors for you.

• *Saturday 25 November* •

Although you're full of seemingly brilliant ideas, how practical are they? Also, are you willing to discuss any criticisms that others may make, or will you fly off the handle? As well as being impractical and impulsive, you may also have a tendency to think you know it all. This makes it difficult for you to benefit from the advice of others and means you may end up shooting yourself in the foot.

• *Sunday 26 November* •

You have the perfect opportunity to win the support of others today. In doing so, you're able to achieve a goal that would otherwise have been beyond you. The reason others help you now is because they're attracted by your sensitivity and humility. They can see that you're not acting from your ego but for the benefit of everyone involved. Doors that were previously closed are now opening for you and success is certain.

• *Monday 27 November* •

Exciting and unexpected opportunities will help you to consolidate your position in the world today. You may also manage to fulfil a cherished goal. Don't be shy about discussing any unusual ideas that come to you, because other people will be intrigued by your original approach. This is no time to hide in the shadows. Be bold and prepare to stake your claim for recognition!

• *Tuesday 28 November* •

You're still in the mood to blow your own trumpet but try not to go OTT. Although you're full of belief in your abilities, you may develop an inflated sense of self-importance which won't impress anyone. You're also unduly optimistic and this could lead to extravagant behaviour that you may regret, probably sooner rather than later. Enjoy the day but make sure you don't take on more than you can handle!

• *Wednesday 29 November* •

A skirmish with a friend seems unavoidable today, and one of you is sure to blow a fuse. The issue is either connected with money or jealousy. Deep emotions that neither of you were aware of come to the surface and leave you both shell-shocked by the anger you both feel. Although it may take a few hours to calm down, you'll end the day even closer than before.

• *Thursday 30 November* •

This is an excellent day for getting your ideas across to others. You're full of curiosity and will happily spend the day in convivial company, speculating upon all manner of things. However, you're also aware of the need to get on with practical tasks that need completing, especially if they include communicating with other people. Try to find time later on for some quiet consideration or meditation. You'll be surprised at how rewarding this will be.

DECEMBER AT A GLANCE

Love	♥ ♥ ♥
Money	£
Career	💻 💻 💻 💻 💻
Health	☼ ☼

• *Friday 1 December* •

Problems in communicating with others ensures that this will be a trying day, although you feel good in yourself. Don't be surprised if a letter or package that you were expecting is delayed. If you need to get hold of someone on the phone, their line is bound to be engaged every time you try them. Even if you do make contact, it may not be a very satisfactory conversation. Don't worry – you'll still achieve your objectives.

• *Saturday 2 December* •

The action that you take today is guaranteed to be constructive and dynamic. You anticipate excitement and adventure, and you'll achieve this because of your positive attitude. The only thing you won't tolerate now is anyone trying to clip your wings and curtail your freedom. This is unlikely to happen, as others appreciate your need to do your own thing at the moment.

• Sunday 3 December •

No matter how much you want to have time to yourself today, family members have other plans. It seems as if they want you to spend time with them. Although you'll be irritated at first, you'll have a much better time than you imagined. Save yourself the bother of an argument and resign yourself to a day of pleasure and indulgence! It's all to do with your state of mind.

• Monday 4 December •

Tread warily at work, as an explosive undercurrent could erupt at any time. You're determined to stand up for yourself and seek the recognition you believe you deserve. Unfortunately, someone with influence has other ideas and will go out of their way to undermine your efforts. Much as it will go against the grain, there's little to be gained from direct confrontation right now. Retire gracefully and bide your time.

• Tuesday 5 December •

After the turbulence of yesterday, you're now in a much better frame of mind and are feeling quite calm and peaceful. An old friend will reassure you of your true worth and make you appreciate the situation from a different perspective. As a result, you're able to resolve any outstanding issues from yesterday and show how willing you are to forgive others, even when they're in the wrong.

• Wednesday 6 December •

As a result of offering the olive branch yesterday, the world now opens up for you. Other people recognize your dignified behaviour and show you how much they respect you for it. Your intuition and ability to visualize ideas will also impress others, and ensure that they'll seek your advice and recognize your excellent qualities. They may also want to share some secret information with you as they know you can be trusted.

• *Thursday 7 December* •

People whose influence is important sang your praises yesterday, but take care not to get too carried away. You don't want this to go to your head, making you overbearing and over-optimistic as a result. Now is the time to apply yourself to your work with a sense of realism, as that is the best way to achieve things now. You should also guard against hypocrisy and making unrealistic promises to anyone at home.

• *Friday 8 December* •

Avoid signing any important documents today if you possibly can. Apart from the fact that someone may be trying to deceive you, you're simply not in the mood to make any sound decisions. Your imagination is boundless at the moment and no doubt you could write some wonderful poetry if you put your mind to it. Don't imagine, however, that your inspiration can be transferred into mundane business affairs or you'll come a cropper!

• *Saturday 9 December* •

Your brilliance and originality will astound everyone around you and ensure that you're able to achieve whatever you want today. Although you are keen to do things your way, others will be happy to fall in alongside you as they know they're in for an exciting ride. You'll also want to show someone at home just how much you care for them. Your philanthropic nature may also extend to people outside the family.

• *Sunday 10 December* •

A card, letter or phone call from a friend reminds you how much you care about them. Life at home seems idyllic, and you'll want to shower your compassion and generosity upon your family. However, no matter how much attention you give to a certain person, they seem determined to soak up every bit of your energy without any consideration for your own needs. Maybe it's time you told them to take responsibility for their own life.

• *Monday 11 December* •

There have been many occasions this year when you have had to juggle the demands of home with your working responsibilities, and you get another crack at the whip over the next two weeks. Although this will cause you some degree of emotional tension, things will fall into place in an unexpected way. This will be a big relief if you're worried about meeting a deadline before the festivities start, and the family keep asking you about your Christmas plans.

• *Tuesday 12 December* •

An extraordinary day lies in store. Your penetrating insight enables you to achieve great things at work. You'll uncover some secret or hidden information and this will make your position stronger than you could possibly imagine. Also, you'll be overwhelmed by a depth of love for someone that you have seldom experienced. Could it be the beginning of a secret affair, or is it simply that you experience feelings towards your family that you've never really noticed before?

• *Wednesday 13 December* •

Don't allow anyone to persuade you into some half-baked financial venture today, even if it means having to lose your temper to make yourself understood! News that you hear later on in the day will prove you right. Although children or a loved one may drive you to distraction, they'll show their appreciation when you give them some advice. Try to set aside some time to consider how you can express more of your creativity.

• *Thursday 14 December* •

Your optimism and positive attitude are exactly what's needed at work because colleagues seem unable to cope at the moment. You may get the flak from them for want of anyone else to blame. Although this initially leaves you feeling hurt and confused, it won't take you long to realize what's really happening. You'll soon weave some magic and restore sanity to the situation. You'll also earn considerable respect at the same time.

• *Friday 15 December* •

Your mind is especially inventive and intuitive today, and will be working at the speed of light. Ideas that come to you will give you great insight into your own behaviour. They'll also help you at work, as you'll see opportunities to increase efficiency, introduce new schemes and generally impress everyone around you. The spin-off here is that you'll prove the value of your contribution, and this can only improve your future prospects.

• *Saturday 16 December* •

This is a day to lounge around the house, preferably with your loved one draped around you! While there's no denying how optimistic and cheerful you feel, and how much you want to indulge yourself, watch out for a couple of pitfalls. First of all, be aware that your good mood may lead you into making promises that you can't deliver. Secondly, you could be feeling in such a party mood that you'll feel very fragile tomorrow!

• *Sunday 17 December* •

You may have to change some existing plans after the news that you hear today. Although this will make you feel irritable and angry, there's no point taking it out on others. Instead, sit down with the people concerned and work out a constructive way to cope with this setback. If you feel stumped, try to approach the situation in an original or highly logical way.

• *Monday 18 December* •

Although a certain person may stand in the way of your plans today, pay them no attention. You're feeling confident and dynamic, and you know what action you need to take in order to achieve your goal. It's an excellent time to push ahead with financial plans, as you can be sure that your judgement is sound. If you feel you're entitled to a pay rise or promotion, now is the time to seek it.

• *Tuesday 19 December* •

It's another good day for pushing ahead with certain goals and staking your claim on the position that you deserve. You'll have plenty of creative ideas for ways to transform your situation at work, and you can be absolutely sure that they'll be well received by people in power or influence. There might also be a secret assignation with someone, or perhaps you are finally prepared to show where your affections lie?

• *Wednesday 20 December* •

Your dynamism is more than obvious to others today, as you show how determined you are to finalize a certain financial deal. You're able to express your views clearly and in a way that makes everyone want to cooperate with you. They can see that what's good for you is also good for them. They'll also be impressed by the depth of your passion, both towards resolving this matter and in other ways too!

• Thursday 21 December •

It's a good idea to be very choosy about who you mix with today. Keep away from anyone who upsets you at the best of times or who is a difficult customer, because they will really get you now. Even though you may be busy with the run-up to Christmas at the moment, you are also starting to think about your long-term hopes and dreams. It's a good time to begin mapping out your strategy for what you want to achieve in 2001.

• Friday 22 December •

This is another day in which you should choose your company carefully because once again there is the possibility of falling out with someone in a big way. Try to avoid committing yourself to any written agreements without reading the small print very carefully first. You should also avoid seeking someone's agreement to a future plan because this isn't a good time to ask for their help.

• Saturday 23 December •

You're feeling wonderfully generous and extravagant today, so it's great for doing some last-minute Christmas shopping – provided you will be sitting down when all the bills arrive. Not that you care about such apparent trivialities today, because you've got the urge to splurge. Besides, you're full of sublime ideas on how to improve your position in the world, so feel you can afford to be indulgent because you'll soon be in the money.

• *Sunday 24 December* •

A successful day is guaranteed because you will achieve all
your objectives thanks to some brilliant planning on your
part. Although you'll want to have some time to yourself, try
not to hide away for too long because all sorts of exciting
possibilities are on the horizon. Maybe you'll meet someone
you haven't seen for a long time. If you're going to a party, you
could encounter exactly the sort of person you would like to
find in your Christmas stocking!

• *Monday 25 December* •

Get set for a lovely Christmas, and one that you will remember
for a long time to come. You're feeling full of energy and want
to have a good time with everyone around you. You're in the
mood to party, and the more people who join you the happier
you'll feel. Don't forget to make a wish when you pull your
cracker because it stands a good chance of coming true over
the next few weeks.

• *Tuesday 26 December* •

A day of calm follows all the excitement of yesterday. The
chances are that you'll need plenty of peace and quiet if you
want to recover from yesterday's fun and frivolity – to say
nothing of all the over-indulgence! Enjoy this chance to be
with people you care about, and try to avoid doing anything
more arduous than deciding which TV programme to watch.
You may not be up for more than that anyway!

• *Wednesday 27 December* •

You have a hankering to be with kindred spirits today, so get
on the phone if you have nothing planned. You're full of good
ideas for things to do, and will have little difficulty in persuad-
ing your friends to fall in with your plans. Indeed, if there are

any old chums that you haven't seen for a while, then make the effort to get in touch with them now and catch up on all the news.

• *Thursday 28 December* •

Although you're full of bright ideas for ways to keep the festivities rolling along at home, you may find that you've bitten off more than you can chew. Someone seems determined to test your patience to the limit, and they will be looking for an opportunity to burst your bubble. You may also have to look after someone who is feeling under the weather or who needs to be pampered.

• *Friday 29 December* •

Much as you'd like to feel free to do your own thing today, circumstances conspire to thwart you. Perhaps you have to put all other plans on hold because you're still looking after someone who needs your support. Whatever has disrupted your day, you'll feel as if you're cut off from the world and this will make you feel lonely and depressed. Try not to take it too much to heart, even though it will be difficult to shake off this gloomy mood.

• *Saturday 30 December* •

After feeling incarcerated for the last two days, you're ready to bolt for freedom! Not that you'll need to, as family members will be happy to encourage you to indulge yourself. You're full of positive thoughts about the future and will want to discuss them with anyone willing to listen. You might even find yourself wandering into a travel agency and walking out with a plane ticket in your hand!

• *Sunday 31 December* •

What have you got planned for today? All you are really interested in is having some fun, preferably surrounded by lots of friends and loved ones. You will adore going to a party or festive gathering, and will do your best to make sure it goes with a swing. Before you get all dolled up, you will enjoy jotting down your New Year resolutions, especially if you are confident that you'll be able to achieve lots of them in 2001. Happy New Year!